Targeting Mental Maths

AUSTRALIAN CURRICULUM EDITION

Garda Turner

PASCAL PRESS

Targeting Mental Maths Year 3
Written by Garda Turner

Updated in 2013 for the Australian Curriculum
Reprinted 2014, 2015, 2016, 2017, 2018, 2019, 2021
Updated in 2022 for the Australian Curriculum
Reprinted 2023, 2025

ISBN 978 1 92288 725 2

Published by Pascal Press
PO Box 250
Glebe NSW 2037
(02) 9198 1748
www.pascalpress.com.au

Publisher: Katy Pike
Series Editor: Garda Turner
Editor: Amanda Santamaria
Designed and typeset by The Modern Art Production Group

Printed by Wai Man Book Binding (China) Ltd.

Contents

Introduction

The importance of mental mathematics

The development of a variety of mental strategies helps to make children confident mathematicians.

Students who can perform mathematical computations swiftly and accurately in their heads are seen as being 'good at maths'. In general, poorer performing students use less efficient strategies and the development of mental computation through a strategy approach can help them move forwards. Research has shown that 'after instruction students seem more likely to use strategies that reflected number sense and that this was a long-term change.' (Markovits and Sowder, 1994)

The Year 3 Targeting Mental Maths book has been written to complement the Targeting Maths Australian Curriculum Year 3 Student Book. The two-page weekly units run parallel to the contents in the student book. Units are divided into four terms of work and each term ends with a Revision Unit. There are 35 units in total.

A unit consists of two facing pages. The left-hand page has three groups of quick mental exercises that constantly practise the necessary maths facts. The right-hand page always starts with an explanation and practice of a mental strategy. This is followed by exercises that include work on space, measurement, position, number, data, chance etc. The page concludes with a Problem of the week.

Students with number sense know the relative size of numbers and use a variety of computation strategies to solve a problem. This enables them to approach maths with a real sense of what they are being asked to do, making them more confident, with a greater ability to work mathematically.

Targeting Mental Maths fulfils the need for easily accessible mental warm-ups, constant practice of maths facts, a useful homework book and further revision of a concept being taught.

Sets A, B and C
The left-hand page has three groups of quick mental exercises that constantly practise the necessary maths facts.

Two-page units
A unit consists of two facing pages.

Mental Strategies
The right-hand page always starts with an explanation and practice of a mental strategy. This structured focus of mental strategies is unique to the Targeting Mental Maths series.

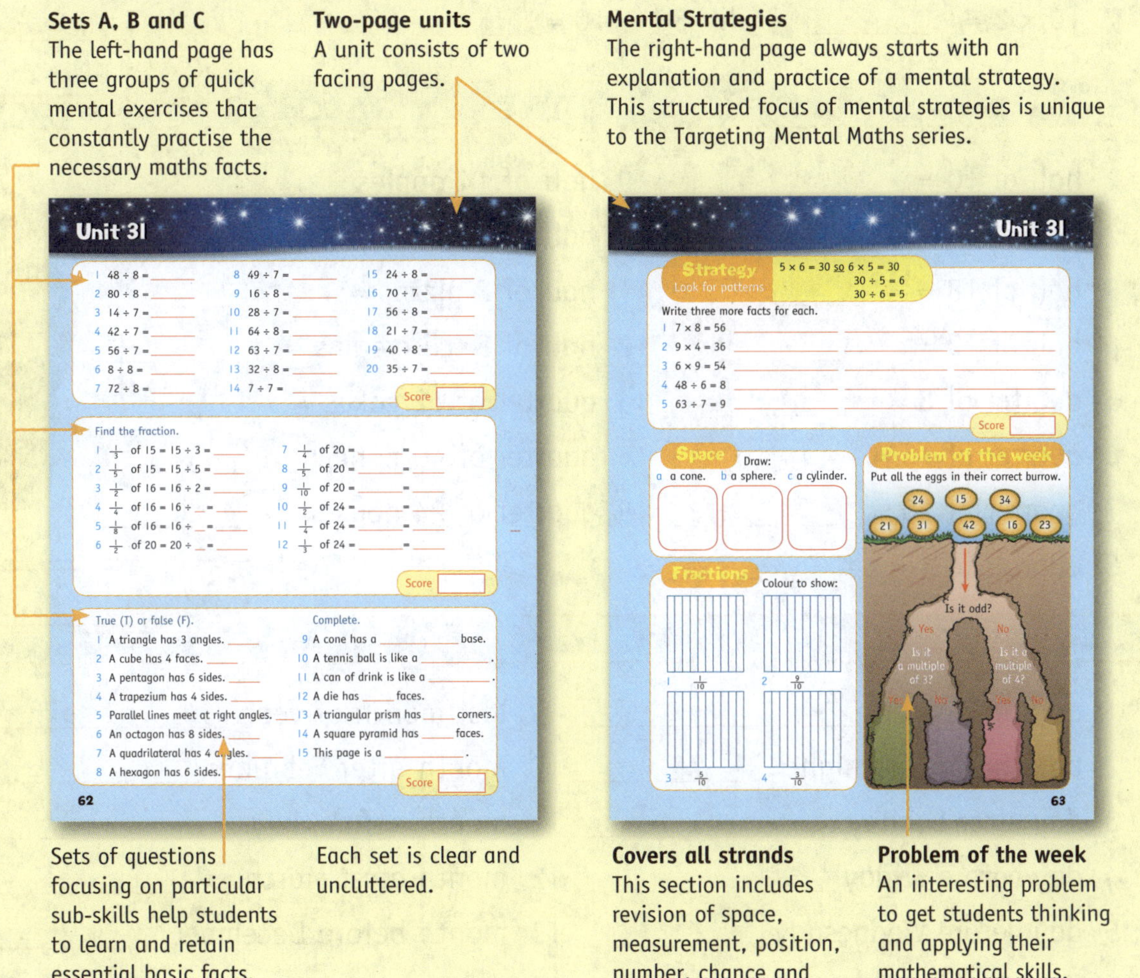

Sets of questions focusing on particular sub-skills help students to learn and retain essential basic facts.

Each set is clear and uncluttered.

Covers all strands
This section includes revision of space, measurement, position, number, chance and data concepts.

Problem of the week
An interesting problem to get students thinking and applying their mathematical skills.

Answers

Answer pages are in the centre of the book so that the complete section can be easily pulled out and kept separate if the teacher so wishes.

Unit 1

A

1 $4 \times 2 =$ ______
2 $5 \times 3 =$ ______
3 $6 \times 5 =$ ______
4 $2 \times 8 =$ ______
5 $7 \times 10 =$ ______
6 $5 \times 1 =$ ______
7 $10 \times 2 =$ ______
8 $8 \div 2 =$ ______
9 $10 \div 5 =$ ______
10 $90 \div 10 =$ ______
11 $12 \div 2 =$ ______
12 $30 \div 5 =$ ______
13 $18 \div 2 =$ ______
14 $30 \div 10 =$ ______
15 $5 \times 5 =$ ______
16 $2 \times 6 =$ ______
17 $0 \times 8 =$ ______
18 $8 \times 5 =$ ______
19 $7 \times 2 =$ ______
20 $5 \times 10 =$ ______

Score ______

B

1 half of 10 = ______
2 half of 6 = ______
3 half of 18 = ______
4 half of 12 = ______
5 quarter of 8 = ______
6 quarter of 16 = ______
7 quarter of 20 = ______
8 quarter of 4 = ______
9 half of 14 apples = ______
10 half of 20 books = ______
11 half of 2 pizzas = ______
12 half of 8 ice-creams = ______
13 quarter of 12 cakes = ______
14 quarter of 40 pencils = ______
15 quarter of 24 dogs = ______

Score ______

C

1 days in 1 week ______
2 days in one fortnight ______
3 day after Sunday ______
4 day before Friday ______
5 day before Wednesday ______
6 day after Monday ______
7 months in 1 year ______
8 first month of year ______
9 last month of year ______
10 month after February ______
11 month before July ______
12 month after March ______
13 month before December ______
14 days in June ______
15 days in January ______

Score ______

Strategy
Making tens

8 + 2 = 10
6 + 4 = 10

18 + 2 = 20
26 + 4 = 30

1 7 + 3 = ______
2 47 + 3 = ______
3 5 + 5 = ______
4 65 + 5 = ______
5 4 + 6 = ______
6 34 + 6 = ______
7 9 + 1 = ______
8 89 + 1 = ______
9 8 + 2 = ______
10 58 + 2 = ______
11 3 + 7 = ______
12 73 + 7 = ______

Score

Space

Top view	Front view	Side view

What's your answer?

You must measure the height of a painting but you don't have a ruler or a measuring tape. How will you do it?

______

______

______

______

______

Problem of the week

A plane has 2 pilots, 3 stewards, 28 people sitting in window seats and 45 people sitting in other seats. How many people are on the full plane?

______

Unit 2

A

ten more than:

1 17 = ______
2 36 = ______
3 181 = ______
4 343 = ______
5 112 = ______
6 428 = ______
7 655 = ______

ten less than:

8 71 = ______
9 64 = ______
10 399 = ______
11 550 = ______
12 217 = ______
13 482 = ______
14 746 = ______

15 34 + 100 = ______
16 573 − 100 = ______
17 925 − 100 = ______
18 359 + 100 = ______
19 770 + 100 = ______
20 838 − 100 = ______

10

Score

B Write each number.

1 one hundred and forty-two ______
2 two hundred and fifteen ______
3 eight hundred and seventy-three ______
4 five hundred and twenty-nine ______
5 six hundred and four ______
6 nine hundred and nineteen ______
7 four hundred and fifty ______
8 seven hundred and thirty-eight ______

Write in order.

9 218, 715, 175 ______ ______ ______
10 301, 97, 258 ______ ______ ______
11 592, 903, 487 ______ ______ ______
12 650, 599, 711 ______ ______ ______
13 281, 812, 182 ______ ______ ______
14 917, 971, 791 ______ ______ ______
15 203, 230, 302 ______ ______ ______

Score

C True or False. (T/F)

1 12 hours in a day. ______
2 4 quarters in one whole . ______
3 My teacher is 1 metre tall. ______
4 A door is about 2 metres tall. ______
5 There are 100c in $1. ______
6 50c = $5 ______
7 Spring has 4 months. ______
8 28 days in 4 weeks. ______
9 My finger is 1 cm long. ______
10 12 eggs in 1 dozen. ______
11 A die has 6 faces. ______
12 60 seconds = 1 minute ______
13 112 is an odd number. ______
14 4th comes after 5th. ______
15 A centimetre is smaller than a metre. ______

Score

Strategy
Near doubles

7 + 8 = 7 + 7 + 1

10 + 9 = 10 + 10 − 1

1 6 + 7 = 6 + 6 + 1 = ______

2 5 + 4 = 5 + 5 − = ______

3 8 + 9 = ______ = ______

4 11 + 10 = ______ = ______

5 4 + 3 = ______ = ______

6 12 + 11 = ______ = ______

7 8 + 7 = ______ = ______

8 20 + 19 = ______ = ______

9 15 + 16 = ______ = ______

Score

Follow directions

Start at ☺

Move:

up 4; left 5;

up 2; right 3;

down 4; right 1;

up 5; left 5;

down 4; right 2;

down 2; left 1

Where did you end up? ______

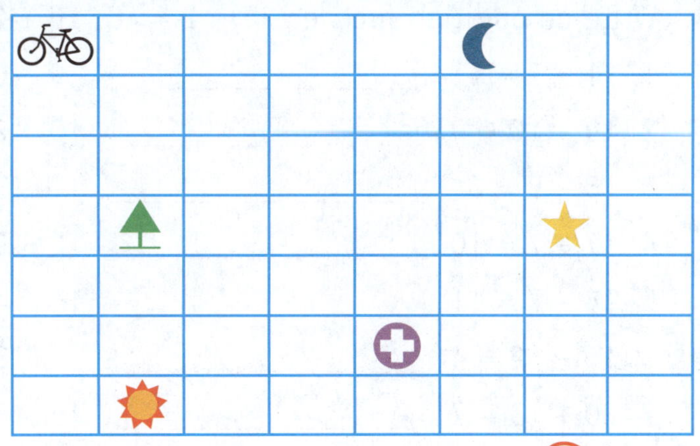

Space

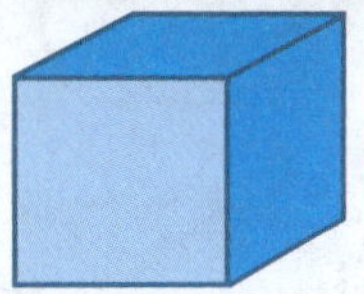

Name	Number of faces	Number of corners	Number of edges

Problem of the week

How many dreams will Grandad have in April? ______

On average people have 4 dreams per night.

Unit 3

A

1. 16 − 7 = ______
2. 12 − 4 = ______
3. 20 − 9 = ______
4. 13 − 7 = ______
5. 18 − 9 = ______
6. 15 − 6 = ______
7. 12 − 8 = ______
8. 14 − 7 = ______
9. 11 − 3 = ______
10. 16 − 5 = ______
11. 12 − 9 = ______
12. 17 − 8 = ______
13. 14 − 5 = ______
14. 16 − 9 = ______
15. 19 − 12 = ______
16. 17 − 5 = ______
17. 13 − 5 = ______
18. 18 − 4 = ______
19. 15 − 8 = ______
20. 10 − 4 = ______

Score

B Write an addition fact. eg 17 − 2 = 15; 15 + 2 = 17

1. 11 − 7 = 4 ______
2. 19 − 10 = 9 ______
3. 15 − 9 = 6 ______
4. 17 − 7 = 10 ______
5. 18 − 7 = 11 ______
6. 16 − 12 = 4 ______
7. 20 − 13 = 7 ______
8. 14 − 9 = 5 ______
9. 16 − 8 = 8 ______
10. 12 − 5 = 7 ______
11. 13 − 9 = 4 ______
12. 19 − 13 = 6 ______
13. 14 − 8 = 6 ______
14. 13 − 2 = 11 ______
15. 17 − 12 = 5 ______

Score

C

1. half of 20 ______
2. quarter of 8 ______
3. half of 16 ______
4. quarter of 4 ______
5. ordinal number after 3rd ______
6. ordinal number before 10th ______
7. even number after 19 ______
8. odd number before 159 ______
9. even number before 26 ______
10. odd number after 32 ______
11. half of 100 ______
12. quarter of 40 ______
13. number after 990 ______
14. number before 2000 ______
15. season before Summer ______

Score

Unit 3

Strategy
Look for patterns

15, 12, 9, 6

Pattern: −3

Write the next term.

1 19, 17, 15, ______

2 8, 12, 16, ______

3 21, 14, 7, ______

4 13, 17, 21, ______

5 3, 11, 19, ______

6 26, 18, 10, ______

7 31, 26, 21, ______

8 15, 19, 23, ______

9 30, 23, 16, ______

10 1, 10, 19, ______

11 40, 31, 22, ______

12 100, 80, 60, ______

Score

Space

Name three things that look like:

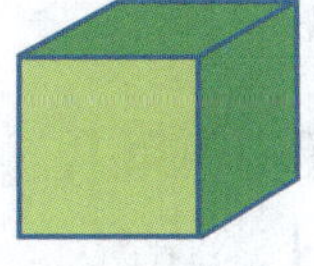

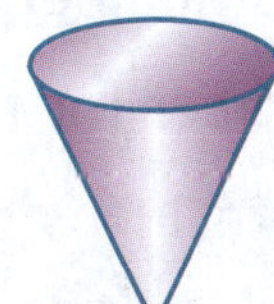

What's your question?

The answer is 7 giraffes.

What is your question?

Problem of the week

Jo-jo had 7 coins. When he added them he found he had exactly $1.

What coins did he have?

Can you think of another group?

Unit 4

A

1. 10 × 6 = ______
2. 2 × 4 = ______
3. 10 × 7 = ______
4. 3 × 5 = ______
5. 4 × 10 = ______
6. 7 × 2 = ______
7. 2 × 5 = ______
8. 5 × 2 = ______
9. 2 × 8 = ______
10. 10 × 1 = ______
11. 6 × 2 = ______
12. 5 × 4 = ______
13. 7 × 5 = ______
14. 5 × 10 = ______
15. 5 × 5 = ______
16. 9 × 5 = ______
17. 9 × 2 = ______
18. 5 × 6 = ______
19. 8 × 5 = ______
20. 10 × 10 = ______

Score

B

1. 2nd number after 16 ______
2. number for three tens ______
3. write 11 as a word ______
4. last number before 20 ______
5. third number after 99 ______
6. number for ten tens ______
7. 10 more than seventy-one ______
8. 10 less than forty-six ______
9. 100 more than fifty-eight ______
10. 100 less than 261 ______
11. seven more than eighteen ______
12. five less than thirty-three ______
13. number before five hundred ______
14. 5th number after 198 ______
15. number between 69 and 71 ______

Score

C Underline the one that holds less.

1. a teaspoon or an eggcup
2. a bucket or a milk jug
3. a bath or a swimming pool
4. a thimble or a cup
5. a can of drink or a carton of milk
6. a teacup or a teapot
7. a coffee mug or a medicine glass
8. a saucepan or a laundry tub

Underline the one that covers more.

9. a book or a newspaper
10. a towel or a blanket
11. a foot or a hand
12. a poster or a birthday card
13. a brick or a door mat
14. a pizza or a biscuit
15. a ruler or a pencil

Score

Unit 4

Strategy

Look for 10s

10

7 + 6 + 3 = 16

1 6 + 4 + 8 = ______

2 5 + 7 + 5 = ______

3 9 + 2 + 8 = ______

4 3 + 4 + 7 = ______

5 6 + 1 + 9 = ______

6 8 + 2 + 8 = ______

7 10 + 9 + 10 = ______

8 12 + 8 + 7 = ______

9 14 + 5 + 6 = ______

10 13 + 25 + 5 = ______

11 7 + 8 + 23 = ______

12 11 + 19 + 6 = ______

Score

Time

What is the time?

1 

:

2 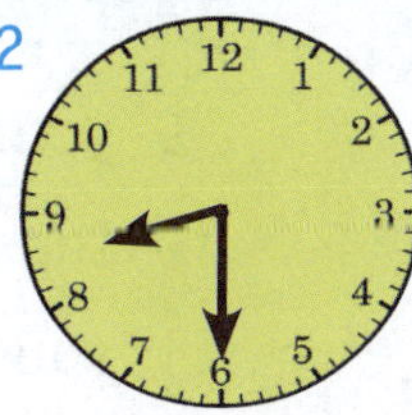

:

3 
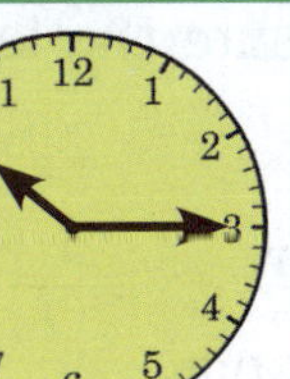

:

4 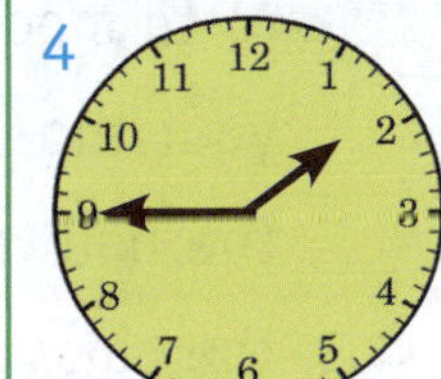

:

Space

Draw:

a cube.

a cylinder.

Problem of the week

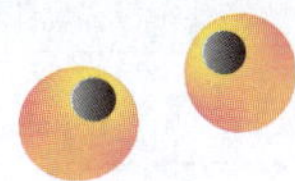
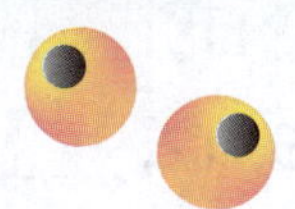

Using only three beads how many different numbers can you make on the abacus? Write the numbers.

______

______

______

Unit 5

A

1 7 + 9 = ______
2 6 + 5 = ______
3 10 + 8 = ______
4 4 + 5 = ______
5 5 + 9 = ______
6 6 + 8 = ______
7 8 + 3 = ______
8 4 + 8 = ______
9 12 + 7 = ______
10 8 + 9 = ______
11 9 + 6 = ______
12 3 + 9 = ______
13 11 + 7 = ______
14 7 + 7 = ______
15 2 + 7 = ______
16 5 + 7 = ______
17 4 + 9 = ______
18 11 + 5 = ______
19 12 + 3 = ______
20 11 + 9 = ______

Score

B Would you use metres (m) or centimetres (cm) to measure the length?

1 your shoe ______
2 the hallway ______
3 the classroom ______
4 a pencil ______
5 a hair ______
6 a large truck ______
7 your thumb ______
8 a swimming pool ______

Estimate the length.

9 your desk ______
10 the door ______
11 your pencil ______
12 the classroom ______
13 your teacher ______
14 your thumb nail ______
15 the window ______

Score

C Use the rule to finish the pattern.

1 + 4 7, 11, ______, ______
2 − 3 15, 12, ______, ______
3 × 2 1, 2, ______, ______
4 halve 24, 12, ______, ______
5 + 9 2, 11, ______, ______
6 − 10 61, 51, ______, ______
7 + 100 3, 103, ______, ______
8 × 5 1, 5, ______, ______

What is the rule?

9 6, 11, 16, 21 ______
10 30, 28, 26, 24 ______
11 40, 20, 10, 5 ______
12 17, 27, 37, 47 ______
13 1, 10, 100, 1 000 ______
14 3, 6, 12, 24 ______
15 52, 43, 34, 25 ______

Score

Unit 5

Strategy

×4 = double, double

7 × 4
7 double = 14
14 double = 28
7 × 4 = 28

1 6 × 4 = ______
2 0 × 4 = ______
3 8 × 4 = ______
4 10 × 4 = ______
5 9 × 4 = ______
6 12 × 4 = ______
7 15 × 4 = ______
8 20 × 4 = ______
9 50 × 4 = ______
10 70 × 4 = ______

Score

Fractions

Colour to match.

1  $\frac{1}{4}$

2 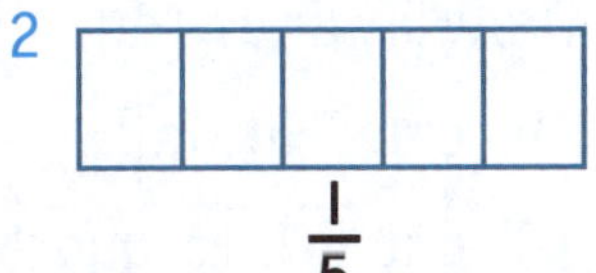 $\frac{1}{5}$

3  $\frac{1}{8}$

4 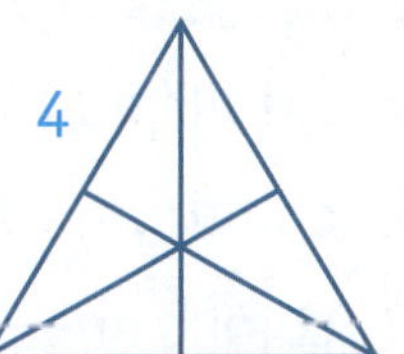 $\frac{1}{6}$

Circle the fraction given.

5 3 out of 8.

6 5 out of 9.

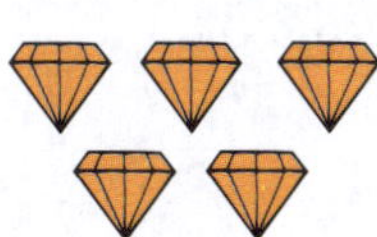

7 2 out of 5.

8 3 out of 6.

Score

Measurement

Measure this line.

Problem of the week

Place these numbers so each side adds to 15.

2 3 5 6 7 10

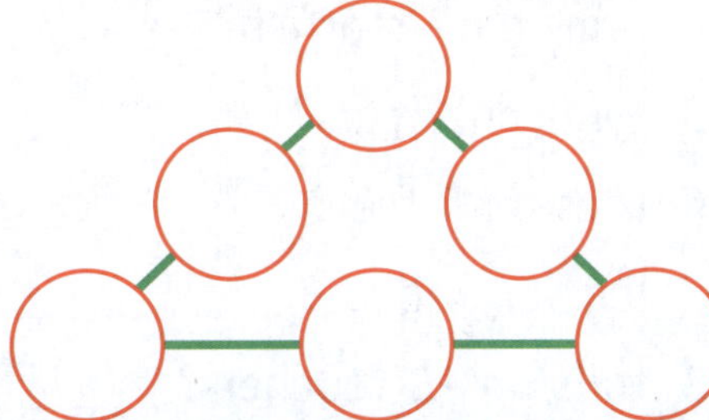

Unit 6

A

1. 4 × 6 = ______
2. 6 × 5 = ______
3. 4 × 5 = ______
4. 4 × 9 = ______
5. 5 × 0 = ______
6. 4 × 4 = ______
7. 5 × 5 = ______
8. 9 × 2 = ______
9. 4 × 0 = ______
10. 10 × 10 = ______
11. 4 × 7 = ______
12. 9 × 5 = ______
13. 4 × 10 = ______
14. 4 × 3 = ______
15. 4 × 1 = ______
16. 3 × 5 = ______
17. 5 × 7 = ______
18. 4 × 8 = ______
19. 3 × 10 = ______
20. 4 × 2 = ______

Score

B

1. colour half of A
2. colour one quarter of B

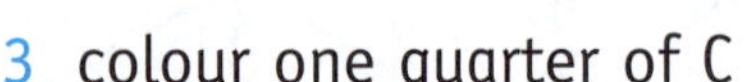

3. colour one quarter of C

4. colour half of D
5. colour one whole of E

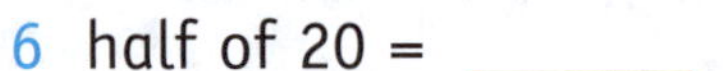

6. half of 20 = ______
7. quarter of 16 = ______
8. quarter of 28 = ______

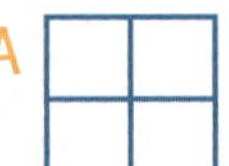

A B C D E

Draw in lines to:

9. cut F in half.

10. cut G into quarters.

11. cut H in half.
12. cut I into quarters.

13. half of 50 = ______

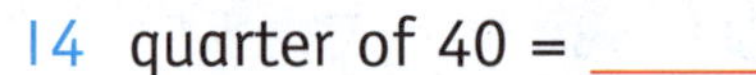

14. quarter of 40 = ______

15. half of 24 = ______

F

G H

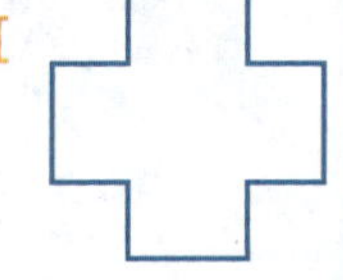

I

Score

C How many:

1. legs on 6 chairs? ______
2. ears on 9 boys? ______
3. eyes on 12 girls? ______
4. arms on 7 starfish? ______
5. tyres on 8 cars? ______
6. toes on 5 feet? ______
7. legs on 4 dogs? ______
8. tails on 10 teachers? ______

Change from $1 if you spend:

9. 50c ______
10. 10c ______
11. 25c ______
12. 40c ______
13. 85c ______
14. $1 ______
15. 65c ______

Score

Unit 6

Strategy

Use a pattern

half of 4 = 2
half of 40 = 20
half of 400 = 200

1 half of 8 = ____
half of 80 = ____
half of 800 = ____

2 quarter of 4 = ____
quarter of 40 = ____
quarter of 400 = ____

3 half of 6 = ____
half of 60 = ____
half of 600 = ____

4 quarter of 8 = ____
quarter of 80 = ____
quarter of 800 = ____

5 half of 10 = ____
half of 100 = ____
half of 1000 = ____

6 quarter of 16 = ____
quarter of 160 = ____
quarter of 1600 = ____

Score

Fractions

Write the fraction for the coloured part.

1 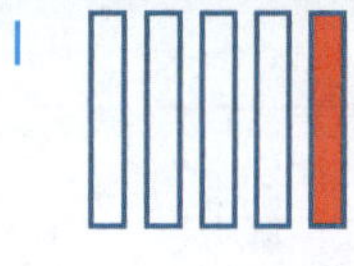
____ fifth

2 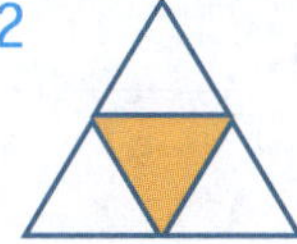
____ quarter

3 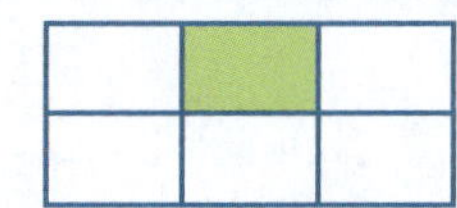
____ sixth

4 
____ eighth

5 
____ ____

6 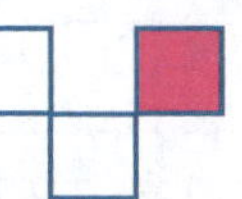 
____ ____

7 
____ ____

8 
____ ____

Score

Problem of the week

Your calculator can spell! Press the numbers 6 6 3. Turn the calculator upside down. It has spelt 'egg'. What do these numbers spell?

1 8078 ____
2 710 ____
3 14 ____
4 3704 ____
5 3507 ____
6 5508 ____
7 8076 ____
8 317 ____
9 35006 ____
10 3705 ____
11 0·7734 ____
12 0·0761 ____

13 Write three number words of your own. ____ ____ ____

Unit 7

A

100 more.

1 76 ______
2 39 ______
3 53 ______
4 64 ______
5 112 ______
6 296 ______
7 403 ______

100 less.

8 617 ______
9 291 ______
10 503 ______
11 999 ______
12 104 ______
13 446 ______
14 838 ______

20 more (+10, +10).

15 72 ______
16 31 ______
17 65 ______
18 137 ______
19 753 ______
20 192 ______

Score

B

Circle the larger number.

1	615	651
2	409	399
3	164	146
4	501	105
5	919	991
6	78	102
7	540	459
8	198	205

Complete.

9 235 = 200 + 30 + ______
10 416 = 400 + ______ + ______
11 198 = ______ + ______ + ______
12 647 = ______ + ______ + ______
13 571 = ______ + ______ + ______
14 350 = ______ + ______ + ______
15 902 = ______ + ______ + ______

Score

C

Make $1.

1 50c + ______
2 20c + ______
3 70c + ______
4 15c + ______
5 35c + ______
6 95c + ______
7 40c + ______
8 65c + ______

9 15c + 45c = ______
10 80c + 15c = ______
11 30c + 25c = ______
12 70c + 20c = ______
13 55c + 25c = ______
14 15c + 85c = ______
15 65c + 35c = ______

Score

Unit 7

Strategy
Look for tens

8 + 13 + 7 = 8 + 20
= 28

Draw a line to link the tens.

1 14 + 9 + 6 = ______

2 8 + 12 + 15 = ______

3 11 + 17 + 3 = ______

4 15 + 9 + 15 = ______

5 21 + 9 + 7 = ______

6 22 + 9 + 8 = ______

7 5 + 6 + 25 = ______

8 17 + 6 + 4 = ______

9 19 + 8 + 11 = ______

10 23 + 18 + 2 = ______

Score

Time

What is the time?

1 
:

2 
:

3 
:

4 
:

5 
:

Score

Views

This is a stove. Draw the:

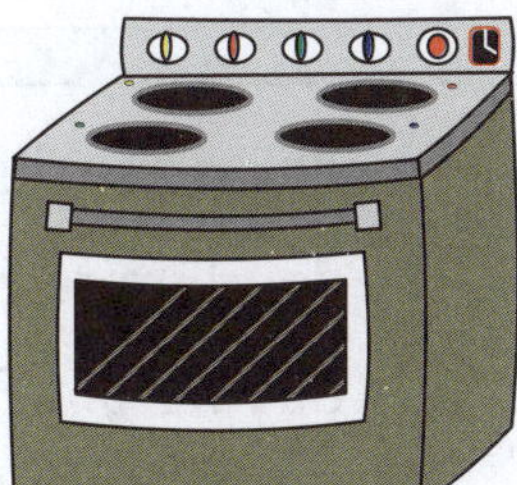

top view.

front view.

side view.

Problem of the week

I am the sixth number in this pattern.

1, 3, 7, 15,

What am I? ______

Unit 8

A

1 20 − 12 = ______

2 13 − 8 = ______

3 17 − 9 = ______

4 15 − 6 = ______

5 20 − 9 = ______

6 12 − 7 = ______

7 14 − 9 = ______

8 20 − 16 = ______

9 13 − 6 = ______

10 17 − 10 = ______

11 18 − 9 = ______

12 14 − 7 = ______

13 20 − 9 = ______

14 16 − 7 = ______

15 12 − 3 = ______

16 15 − 12 = ______

17 18 − 4 = ______

18 16 − 5 = ______

19 15 − 8 = ______

20 19 − 9 = ______

Score

B Write in words.

1 84 ______

2 316 ______

3 128 ______

4 710 ______

5 542 ______

6 811 ______

7 999 ______

8 204 ______

9 670 ______

10 19 ______

Score

C

1 minutes in one hour = ______

2 minutes in $\frac{1}{2}$ hour = ______

3 minutes in $\frac{1}{4}$ hour = ______

4 minutes in $\frac{3}{4}$ hour = ______

5 minutes in 2 hours = ______

6 hours in 1 day = ______

7 days in 1 week = ______

8 months in 1 year = ______

9 day after Sunday ______

10 day before Saturday ______

11 day before Friday ______

12 day after Friday ______

13 days in 1 fortnight ______

14 1st month of the year ______

15 last month of the year ______

Score

Unit 8

Strategy

×10 → add a zero eg 19 × 10 = 190
×20 → double and add a zero
eg 14 × 20 = (14 × 2)0 = 280

1 16 × 10 = ______	6 79 × 10 = ______	11 8 × 20 = ______
2 13 × 10 = ______	7 46 × 10 = ______	12 5 × 20 = ______
3 11 × 10 = ______	8 92 × 10 = ______	13 11 × 20 = ______
4 25 × 10 = ______	9 9 × 20 = ______	14 13 × 20 = ______
5 31 × 10 = ______	10 6 × 20 = ______	15 15 × 20 = ______

Score

Space

Name these prisms.

1 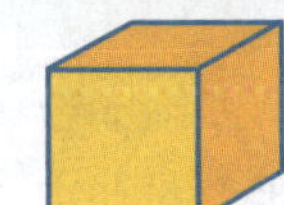 ______

2 ______

3  ______

4  ______

Name these pyramids.

5 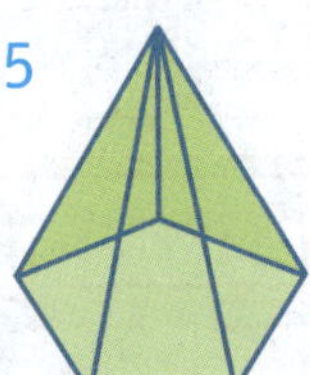 ______

6 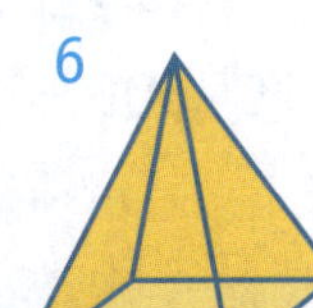 ______

7 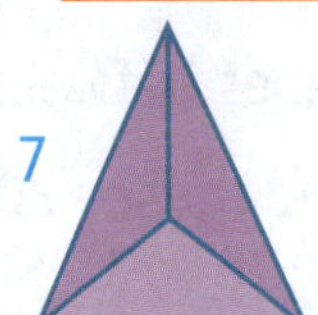 ______

Score

Chance

Write something that:

1 is certain to happen. ______
2 is unlikely to happen. ______
3 definitely will not happen. ______

Problem of the week

How can 8 leave 3 if you take half away? ______

Unit 9 Revision

A

1 2 × 8 = ______
2 5 × 7 = ______
3 4 × 6 = ______
4 9 × 10 = ______
5 8 × 4 = ______
6 4 × 0 = ______
7 76 + 10 = ______
8 213 + 100 = ______
9 649 − 100 = ______
10 361 − 10 = ______
11 20 − 9 = ______
12 16 − 7 = ______
13 8 + 5 = ______
14 4 + 9 = ______
15 11 + 8 = ______
16 15 − 6 = ______
17 60 + 20 = ______
18 37 + 20 = ______
19 4 × 7 = ______
20 9 × 5 = ______

Score

B

1 half of 16 = ______
2 half of 12 = ______
3 quarter of 8 = ______
4 quarter of 20 = ______
5 circle the larger 196, 503
6 circle the smaller 220, 119
7 number between 199 and 201 ______
8 order these. 203, 302, 195

______ ______ ______

Write the number.

9 three hundred and seventeen ______
10 eight hundred and six ______
11 five less than forty-three ______
12 4th number after 97 ______
13 273 = ______ + ______ + ______
14 918 = ______ + ______ + ______
15 605 = ______ + ______ + ______

Score

C

1 month before July ______
2 days in April ______
3 + 7 11, 18, 25, ______
4 − 9 42, 33, 24, ______
5 Cost 55c. Change from $1. ______
6 25c + 65c = ______
7 minutes in $\frac{3}{4}$ of an hour ______
8 1 dozen = ______

True (T) or False (F).

9 4 quarters in 1 whole. ______
10 114 is an odd number. ______
11 A m is smaller than a cm. ______
12 11th comes before 12th. ______
13 A bath holds less than a bucket. ______
14 A hand covers more than a blanket. ______
15 20 days in a fortnight. ______

Score

Revision

Strategy

Use the strategies you have learnt.

1 46 + 4 = ______

2 20 + 19 = ______

3 15 + 16 = ______

4 7 + 9 + 3 = ______

5 13 + 6 + 4 = ______

6 half of 6 = ______

half of 60 = ______

half of 600 = ______

7 half of 18 = ______

half of 180 = ______

half of 1800 ______

8 15 × 4 = ______

9 22 × 4 = ______

10 73 × 10 = ______

11 56 × 10 = ______

12 23 × 20 = ______

Score

Space

Draw:

a cube.

a cone.

a triangle.

a circle.

Fractions

Colour to match.

1  $\frac{1}{4}$

2  $\frac{1}{2}$

3  $\frac{1}{5}$

4 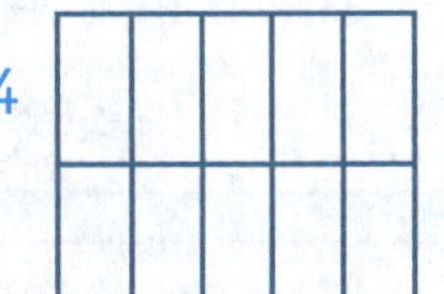 $\frac{1}{10}$

Time

On the digital clock write the time 5 minutes later.

1 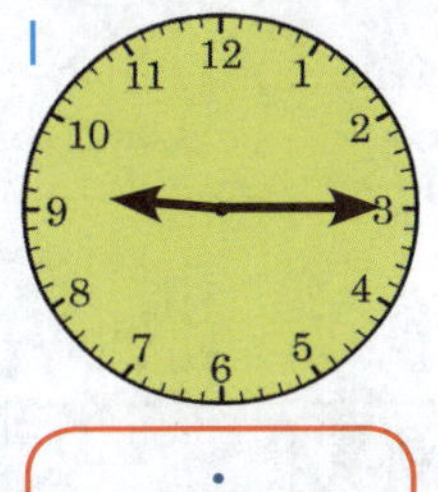

:

2 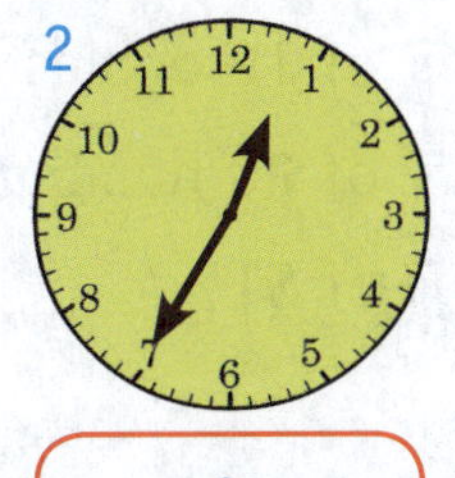

:

Measurement

1 Draw something which is about 5 cm long.

2 Draw something which is about 1 m long.

Unit 10

A

1 11 + 9 = ______
2 8 + 12 = ______
3 13 + 6 = ______
4 5 + 14 = ______
5 16 + 3 = ______
6 7 + 12 = ______
7 9 + 8 = ______
8 20 − 13 = ______
9 20 − 11 = ______
10 20 − 8 = ______
11 20 − 3 = ______
12 20 − 18 = ______
13 20 − 6 = ______
14 20 − 5 = ______
15 18 − 9 = ______
16 15 − 7 = ______
17 13 − 6 = ______
18 19 − 12 = ______
19 16 − 9 = ______
20 17 − 11 = ______

Score

B What is the value of:

1 the 7 in 67? ______
2 the 3 in 39? ______
3 the 4 in 456? ______
4 the 1 in 971? ______
5 the 5 in 853? ______
6 the 8 in 718? ______
7 the 6 in 609? ______
8 the 0 in 508? ______

Write in numerals.

9 eighty-three ______
10 two hundred and twenty-eight ______
11 five hundred and forty-one ______
12 seven hundred and nineteen ______
13 three hundred and seven ______
14 nine hundred and twelve ______
15 six hundred and seventy ______

Score

C

1 2 cakes at 70c. ______
2 3 books at $4 each. ______
3 Spent 75c. Change from $1. ______
4 Spent 15c. Change from $1. ______
5 Spent $1.40. Change from $2. ______
6 How many 10c coins make $1? ______
7 How many 20c coins make $1? ______
8 How many 5c coins make 50c? ______
9 $\frac{1}{2}$ a year = ______ months
10 $\frac{1}{4}$ of an hour = ______ minutes
11 $\frac{1}{2}$ a dozen = ______
12 $\frac{1}{4}$ of $1 = ______
13 $\frac{1}{3}$ of 12 apples = ______
14 $\frac{1}{5}$ of 20 hamburgers = ______
15 $\frac{1}{10}$ of $1 = ______

Score

Unit 10

Strategy
Look for patterns

eg 7 + 6 = 1<u>3</u>
17 + 6 = 2<u>3</u>
37 + 6 = 4<u>3</u>

1 8 + 5 = ______
18 + 5 = ______

2 9 + 7 = ______
19 + 7 = ______

3 4 + 3 = ______
14 + 3 = ______

4 5 + 9 = ______
15 + 9 = ______

5 8 + 4 = ______
18 + 4 = ______

6 6 + 8 = ______
16 + 8 = ______

7 3 + 8 = ______
23 + 8 = ______

8 9 + 9 = ______
39 + 9 = ______

9 6 + 5 = ______
46 + 5 = ______

Score

Abacus
What numbers are shown?

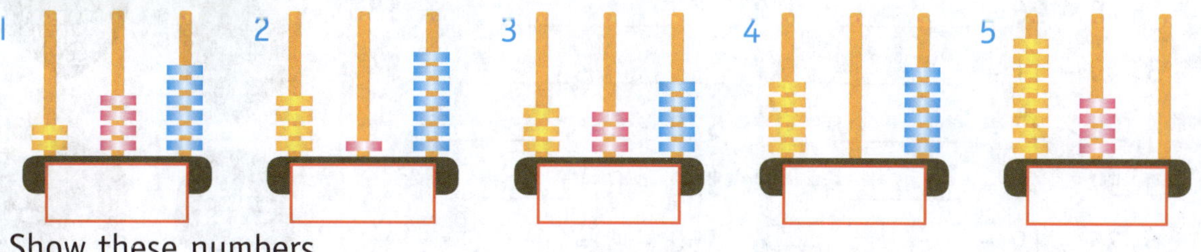

Show these numbers.

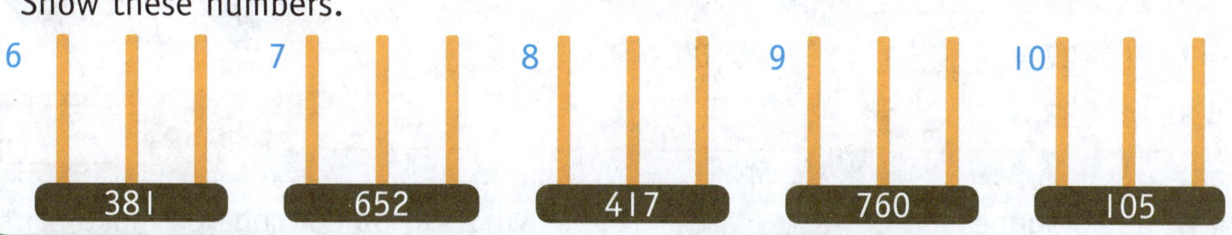

Chance
You throw a die.

1 What numbers could you throw?

______

2 How many possible outcomes are there?

______

Space
What 3D object do these faces make?

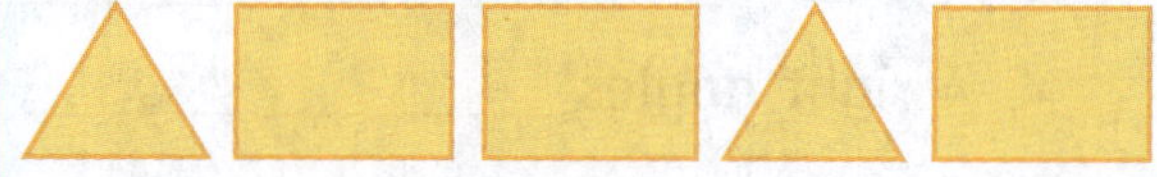

______

Problem of the week
Make nine by adding 5 lines to these six lines. | | | | | |

Unit 11

A

1 11 − 7 = ______
2 20 − 9 = ______
3 18 − 9 = ______
4 12 − 9 = ______
5 11 − 3 = ______
6 15 − 6 = ______
7 17 − 9 = ______
8 18 − 15 = ______
9 12 − 5 = ______
10 13 − 6 = ______
11 16 − 8 = ______
12 19 − 13 = ______
13 14 − 9 = ______
14 16 − 9 = ______
15 15 − 7 = ______
16 17 − 11 = ______
17 13 − 8 = ______
18 14 − 7 = ______
19 20 − 12 = ______
20 19 − 8 = ______

Score

B Estimate only.

1 63 − 41 = ______
2 78 − 26 = ______
3 49 − 11 = ______
4 92 − 27 = ______
5 57 − 41 = ______
6 35 − 19 = ______
7 81 − 27 = ______
8 74 − 33 = ______

Which masks?

9  ______ + ______ = $40
10  ______ + ______ = $36
11  ______ + ______ = $42
12 $20 − C = ______
13 $50 − B = ______
14 $50 − A = ______
15 $100 − D = ______

A

B

C $17

D $15

Score

C What 2D shape?

1 4 equal sides ______
2 3 sides ______
3 5 sides ______
4 4 right angles ______
5 6 sides ______
6 2 equal sides ______
7 3 angles ______
8 8 angles ______

What 3D object can you make using:

9 4 triangles? ______
10 6 squares? ______
11 2 triangles + 3 rectangles? ______
12 4 triangles + 1 square? ______

Score

Strategy

Counting on for subtraction

43 – 37 (38, 39, 40, 41, 42, 43) = 6

Count on to complete.

1

	32	38	35	39	36	31
–29						

2

	51	48	54	52	47	50
–43						

Score

Space

A 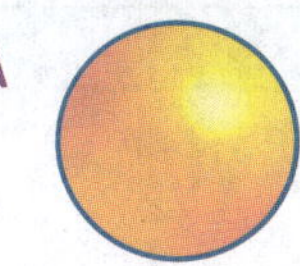

B

C 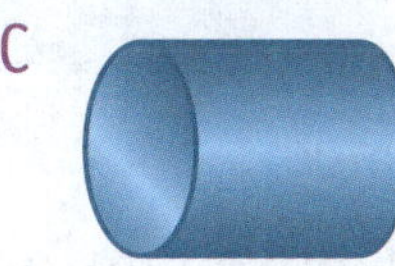

1 Name: A ______________ B ______________ C ______________

2 View from top.

A	B	C

3 View from front.

A	B	C

Calculator

In how many ways can you make 100 without using any digit more than once? eg 98 + 2

Problem of the week

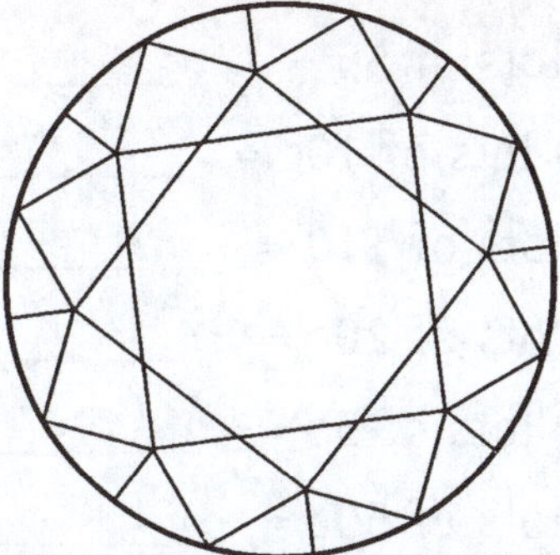

Use 4 colours to colour this shape. Shapes that share a side cannot be the same colour.

Unit 12

A

1 6 + 8 − 7 = ______
2 11 − 4 + 5 = ______
3 3 + 8 − 4 = ______
4 17 − 9 + 5 = ______
5 15 − 5 + 6 = ______
6 8 + 5 − 6 = ______
7 13 − 4 + 9 = ______
8 9 + 7 − 5 = ______
9 20 − 12 + 8 = ______
10 4 + 9 − 8 = ______
11 10 + 6 − 12 = ______
12 14 − 6 + 11 = ______
13 5 + 7 − 4 = ______
14 16 − 4 + 7 = ______
15 6 + 6 − 2 = ______
16 18 − 13 + 9 = ______
17 20 − 7 + 6 = ______
18 7 + 8 − 9 = ______
19 15 − 7 + 4 = ______
20 13 − 6 + 12 = ______

Score

B What is the number?

1 two hundreds, five tens and seven ones ______
2 six tens, nine hundreds and four ones ______
3 two ones, three tens and eight hundreds ______
4 nine tens, five ones and six hundreds ______
5 one hundred, six ones and four tens ______
6 three ones, three hundreds and seven tens ______
7 eight ones and five hundreds ______
8 two tens and nine hundreds ______

Score

C

1 4 lots of $5 = ______
2 10 lots of 10c = ______
3 7 lots of $10 = ______
4 9 lots of 20c = ______
5 20 lots of 5c = ______
6 8 lots of 50c = ______
7 5 lots of $20 = ______
8 6 lots of $50 = ______
9 6 lots of 4 ______
10 difference between 13 and 9 ______
11 the sum of 7 and 12 ______
12 take 11 from 30 ______
13 total 5, 8 and 9 ______
14 minus 13 from 25 ______
15 ten lots of half of 10 ______

Score

Unit 12

Strategy
Related facts

9 – 7 = 2 <u>so</u> 9 – 2 = 7 ; 7 + 2 = 9 ; 2 + 7 = 9

Write three related facts for each.

1 12 – 7 = 5 ______ ______ ______

2 19 – 13 = 6 ______ ______ ______

3 15 – 8 = 7 ______ ______ ______

4 7 + 9 = 16 ______ ______ ______

5 6 + 7 = 13 ______ ______ ______

Score

Chance

Write *certain* (C), *likely* (L) or *impossible* (I).

1 The dog will have two fins. ______

2 The teacher is 2 years old. ______

3 A baby will be born today. ______

4 It will rain next week. ______

5 The puppy is a boy dog. ______

Measurement

Draw a zig-zag line 15 cm long.

Direction

CRAZY
MATHS

What letter:

1 is above T? ______

2 is below R? ______

3 is next to S? ______

4 is before Y? ______

5 is under A? ______

6 is on top of M? ______

7 is after C? ______

8 is diagonal to C? ______

Problem of the week

I pay a dentist's bill of $190 using 6 notes.

Which notes did I use?

______

______

______

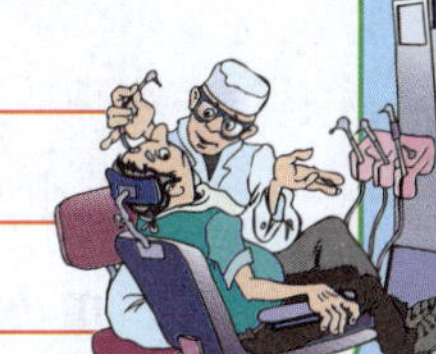

Unit 13

A

1 4 × 0 = ______
2 2 × 7 = ______
3 5 × 9 = ______
4 4 × 3 = ______
5 2 × 9 = ______
6 4 × 5 = ______
7 5 × 5 = ______
8 4 × 9 = ______
9 2 × 6 = ______
10 5 × 8 = ______
11 4 × 4 = ______
12 5 × 6 = ______
13 10 × 10 = ______
14 2 × 5 = ______
15 5 × 7 = ______
16 4 × 6 = ______
17 10 × 0 = ______
18 4 × 7 = ______
19 10 × 3 = ______
20 4 × 8 ______

Score

B

What is the value of:

1 7 in 67 ______
2 3 in 31 ______
3 5 in 502 ______
4 9 in 398 ______
5 4 in 724 ______
6 8 in 863 ______
7 6 in 962 ______
8 0 in 406 ______

Write in words.

9 27 ______
10 43 ______
11 19 ______
12 78 ______
13 11 ______
14 12 ______
15 406 ______

Score

C

Circle the larger.

1 2 weeks or 1 month
2 50 cm or 1 m
3 2 min or 20 seconds
4 1 year or 8 months
5 5 tens or 49
6 265 cents or $3
7 30 days or 3 weeks
8 2 m or 30 cm

How many?

9 minutes in 60 seconds ______
10 days in 48 hours ______
11 weeks in 21 days ______
12 metres in 300 cm ______
13 years in 36 months ______
14 days in May ______
15 days in 1 fortnight ______

Score

Unit 13

Strategy
Multiplying by 5

add a zero and halve
eg $16 \times 5 = 160 \div 2$
$= 80$

1 $13 \times 5 =$ 130 ÷ 2
$=$ ______

2 $17 \times 5 =$ ______
$=$ ______

3 $19 \times 5 =$ ______
$=$ ______

4 $14 \times 5 =$ ______
$=$ ______

5 $12 \times 5 =$ ______
$=$ ______

6 $18 \times 5 =$ ______
$=$ ______

7 $15 \times 5 =$ ______
$=$ ______

8 $22 \times 5 =$ ______
$=$ ______

Score

Fractions

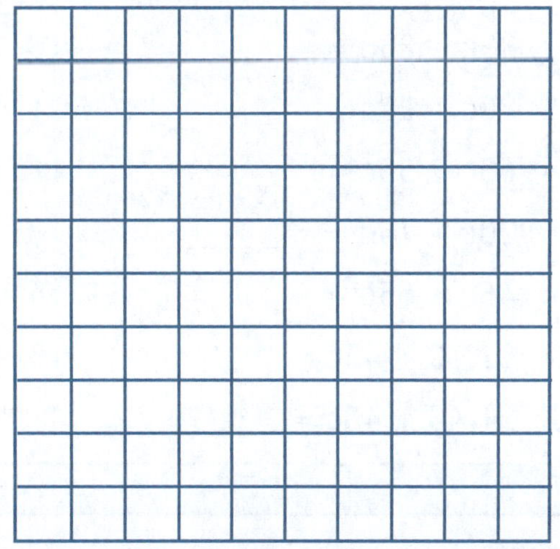

Colour:

- $\frac{1}{4}$ yellow
- $\frac{1}{8}$ blue
- $\frac{3}{10}$ red
- $\frac{1}{5}$ green.

What fraction remains white? ______

Problem of the week

- Think of a number. ______
- Add 3 to it. ______
- Double the answer. ______
- Subtract 4. ______
- Divide the answer in half. ______
- Subtract the number you first thought of. ______

- Your answer should be 1.
- Try it again with a different number.
- Give the instructions to your family.
- They will think you have magical powers when you tell them the answer is 1.

Unit 14

A

1 7 + 6 + 9 = ______
2 3 + 8 + 2 = ______
3 6 + 7 + 5 = ______
4 4 + 6 + 9 = ______
5 9 + 7 + 3 = ______
6 8 + 8 + 6 = ______
7 4 + 8 + 7 = ______
8 2 + 9 + 7 = ______
9 5 + 7 + 9 = ______
10 9 + 8 + 6 = ______
11 7 + 7 + 8 = ______
12 9 + 6 + 7 = ______
13 9 + 6 + 9 = ______
14 5 + 8 + 6 = ______
15 7 + 8 + 4 = ______
16 8 + 2 + 7 = ______
17 5 + 9 + 3 = ______
18 9 + 9 + 5 = ______
19 5 + 6 + 8 = ______
20 7 + 9 + 7 = ______

Score

B

1 50c + 60c = ______
2 35c + 25c = ______
3 80c + 20c = ______
4 60c + 50c = ______
5 20c + 75c = ______
6 45c + 65c = ______
7 $1.10 + 45c = ______
8 $1.40 + 45c = ______
9 $1.15 + 50c = ______
10 $1.80 + 40c = ______
11 $1.75 + 60c = ______
12 $2.05 + 35c = ______
13 $2.25 + 75c = ______
14 $2.50 + 65c = ______
15 $2.80 + $1.20 = ______

Score

C Write to the nearest 5c.

1 11c ______

2 28c ______

3 93c ______

4 42c ______
5 76c ______
6 84c ______
7 39c ______
8 57c ______

Write to the nearest dollar.

9 $1.15 ______

10 $1.65 ______
11 $2.80 ______
12 $3.25 ______
13 $8.75 ______
14 $4.60 ______
15 $9.45 ______

Score

Strategy

Split strategy for subtraction

eg 37 – 19 = 27 – 10 – 9
= 18

1 25 – 16 = 25 - 10 - 6 ____________
= ________

2 35 – 23 = ____________________
= ________

3 74 – 26 = ____________________
= ________

4 58 – 35 = ____________________
= ________

5 41 – 25 = ____________________
= ________

6 32 – 17 = ____________________
= ________

7 27 – 19 = ____________________
= ________

8 53 – 36 = ____________________
= ________

Score

At the Fair

How much to buy and how much change from $10?

1 a bear + panda? ______________ b Change ________

2 a ball + puppet? ______________ b Change ________

3 a puppet + panda? ______________ b Change ________

4 a ball + bear? ______________ b Change ________

5 a all four items? ______________ b Change ________

$1.80

$2.20

Calculator

Enter the number 3 074 on your calculator. In one move how do you change it to:

1 3004? ____________________

2 1074? ____________________

3 3024? ____________________

4 2574? ____________________

Problem of the week

Many countries have their own money.

Find the main unit of money used in:

1 Fiji ____________

2 England ____________

3 Vietnam ____________

4 Thailand ____________

5 Japan ____________

6 Indonesia ____________

7 India ____________

8 Malaysia ____________

Unit 15

A

1. 3 × 3 = ______
2. 3 × 8 = ______
3. 3 × 5 = ______
4. 3 × 9 = ______
5. 3 × 7 = ______
6. 0 × 3 = ______
7. 3 × 4 = ______
8. 10 × 3 = ______
9. 3 × 6 = ______
10. 1 × 3 = ______
11. 2 × 3 = ______

Score

B True or false?

1. 2 quarters = 1 whole ______
2. 3 thirds = 1 whole ______
3. 4 eighths = 1 half ______
4. 5 tenths = 1 whole ______
5. 4 fifths = 1 whole ______
6. 3 sixths = 1 half ______
7. 5 tenths = 1 half ______
8. 8 eighths = 1 whole ______

Score

C How many faces?

1. a cube ______
2. a rectangular prism ______
3. a triangular pyramid ______
4. a square pyramid ______
5. a pentagonal prism ______

How many corners?

6. a cube ______
7. a square pyramid ______
8. a triangular prism ______

Write the time.

9. 5 min after 1 o'clock ______
10. 10 min after 6:30 ______
11. 5 mins before 7:10 ______
12. 15 mins after 8 o'clock ______
13. 5 min before 2 o'clock ______
14. 15 min before 9:30 ______
15. 1 min after 10 o'clock ______

Score

Unit 15

Strategy

×4 — double, double

13 × 4 = 13 double (26) double (52) = 52

1	12 × 4 = ______	5	22 × 4 = ______	9	42 × 4 = ______
2	30 × 4 = ______	6	50 × 4 = ______	10	60 × 4 = ______
3	15 × 4 = ______	7	40 × 4 = ______	11	16 × 4 = ______
4	25 × 4 = ______	8	21 × 4 = ______	12	14 × 4 = ______

Score

Patterns

Here are three Number Changing Factories.

A: In → × 3 →

B: In → − 4 →

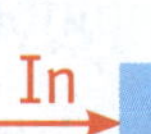

C: In → + 11 →

What do these numbers become when they enter each factory?

	Number	A	B	C
1	8			
2	10			
3	4			
4	7			

	Number	A	B	C
5	20			
6	30			
7	100			
8	50			

Score

Capacity

1 Name 4 things which can be measured in millilitres.

______ ______

______ ______

2 Name 4 things which can be measured in litres.

______ ______

______ ______

Problem of the week

Jessie had 7 pets. She had horses, ducks and spiders. Altogether they had 30 legs.

How many of each pet did she own?

______

______

______

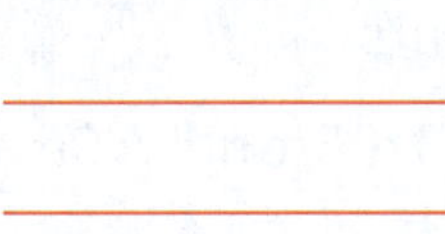

Unit 16

A

1 7 + 6 − 3 = ______
2 8 − 5 + 9 = ______
3 4 + 7 + 8 = ______
4 9 − 4 + 7 = ______
5 3 + 7 − 8 = ______
6 11 − 9 + 10 = ______
7 4 + 8 + 5 = ______
8 13 − 7 − 5 = ______
9 19 − 9 + 3 = ______
10 15 + 2 − 9 = ______
11 16 − 8 − 8 = ______
12 14 − 5 + 6 = ______
13 7 + 8 + 5 = ______
14 3 + 9 − 2 = ______
15 20 − 14 − 5 = ______
16 13 + 3 − 7 = ______
17 5 + 8 − 10 = ______
18 19 − 12 − 4 = ______
19 7 + 6 + 7 = ______
20 9 + 8 − 11 = ______

Score

B Write the next number.

1 2, 4, 6, ______
2 4, 8, 12, ______
3 20, 17, 14, ______
4 5, 10, 15, ______
5 11, 18, 25, ______
6 40, 31, 22, ______
7 7, 70, 700, ______
8 2, 4, 8, ______
9 $\frac{1}{5}$, $\frac{2}{5}$, $\frac{3}{5}$, ______
10 $\frac{7}{8}$, $\frac{6}{8}$, $\frac{5}{8}$, ______
11 $\frac{1}{2}$, $\frac{1}{3}$, $\frac{1}{4}$, ______
12 0, 9, 18, ______
13 97, 87, 77, ______
14 80, 40, 20, ______

Score

C How many?

1 days in 2 weeks ______
2 seconds in 2 min ______
3 minutes in $\frac{1}{4}$ hour ______
4 hours in 1 day ______
5 hours between noon and 7 pm ______
6 minutes in $1\frac{1}{2}$ hours ______
7 seconds between 7:05 and 7:06 ______
8 days in 6 weeks ______

Make 1 litre.

9 500 mL + ______
10 900 mL + ______
11 300 mL + ______
12 700 mL + ______
13 200 mL + ______
14 600 mL + ______
15 1000 mL + ______

Score

Unit 16

Strategy
Near doubles

15 + 16 = 15 + 15 + 1 or 9 + 10 = 10 + 10 − 1
= 31 = 19

1 14 + 13 = ______
2 20 + 19 = ______
3 13 + 12 = ______
4 29 + 30 = ______
5 11 + 12 = ______
6 40 + 39 = ______
7 26 + 25 = ______
8 50 + 49 = ______
9 15 + 14 = ______
10 69 + 70 = ______
11 51 + 50 = ______
12 80 + 79 = ______
13 31 + 30 = ______
14 19 + 21 = ______
15 99 + 99 = ______

Score

Time sequence

In which order do these happen in a day? Order them from 1 – 10.

Feed the dog. ______
Eat dinner. ______
Do my homework. ______
Watch TV. ______
Make my bed. ______
Play with my friend. ______
Make my lunch. ______
Read my book. ______
Have a bath or a shower. ______
Clean my teeth. ______

Space

Colour:
triangles red
quadrilaterals blue
pentagons yellow
hexagons green
octagons purple

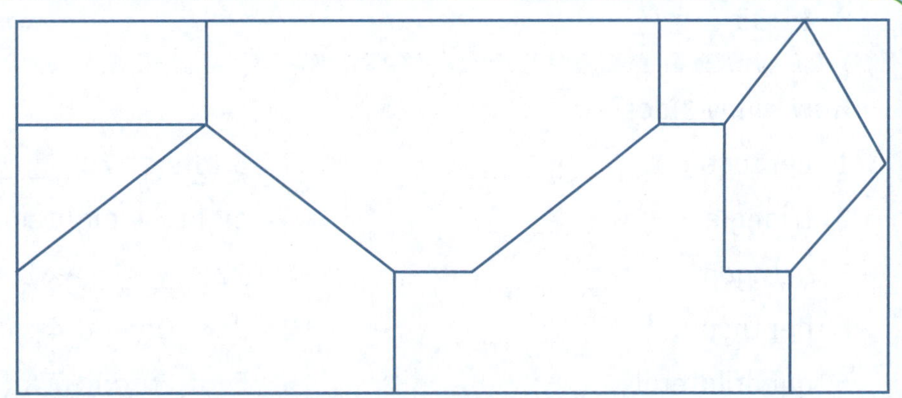

Problem of the week

Yesterday my baby brother had 4 naps for 4 hr 20 min, 2 hr 40 min, 2 hr 35 min and 5 hr 50 min. How long was he awake? ______

Unit 17

A

1 16 − 9 = ______
2 36 − 9 = ______
3 4 + 7 = ______
4 14 + 7 = ______
5 15 − 8 = ______
6 65 − 8 = ______
7 9 + 5 = ______
8 39 + 5 = ______
9 11 − 3 = ______
10 51 − 3 = ______
11 8 + 6 = ______
12 78 + 6 = ______
13 4 + 9 = ______
14 44 + 9 = ______
15 13 − 6 = ______
16 43 − 6 = ______
17 7 + 9 = ______
18 87 + 9 = ______
19 19 − 12 = ______
20 99 − 12 = ______

Score

B Change from $2.

1 $1.50 ______
2 $1.80 ______
3 $1.75 ______
4 $1.25 ______
5 80c ______
6 15c ______
7 95c ______
8 $1.35 ______

Circle the smaller.

9 $\frac{5}{10}$ $\frac{3}{10}$
10 $\frac{5}{6}$ $\frac{6}{6}$
11 $\frac{4}{8}$ $\frac{7}{8}$
12 $\frac{3}{5}$ $\frac{5}{5}$
13 1 whole $\frac{3}{4}$
14 $\frac{1}{2}$ $\frac{1}{4}$
15 $\frac{1}{2}$ $\frac{3}{4}$

Score

C How many sides?

1 pentagon ______
2 triangle ______
3 octagon ______
4 heptagon ______
5 quadrilateral ______
6 hexagon ______

How many angles?

7 octagon ______
8 pentagon ______

9 5 lots of 7 ______
10 eighty + eighteen ______
11 12 = ______ × 3
12 2 × 10c and 4 × 20c ______
13 $\frac{1}{2}$ of 20 and $\frac{1}{4}$ of 8 ______
14 one hundred − 2 lots of 6 ______
15 15 more than 17 ______

Score

Unit 1

A 1 8 2 15 3 30 4 16
5 70 6 5 7 20 8 4
9 2 10 9 11 6 12 6
13 9 14 3 15 25 16 12
17 40 18 40 19 14 20 50

B 1 5 2 3 3 9 4 6
5 2 6 4 7 5 8 1
9 7 10 10 11 1 12 4
13 3 14 10 15 6

C 1 7 2 14 3 Monday
4 Thursday 5 Tuesday
6 Tuesday 7 12
8 January 9 December
10 March 11 June
12 April 13 November
14 30 15 31

Strategy
1 10 2 50 3 10 4 70
5 10 6 40 7 10 8 90
9 10 10 60 11 10 12 80

Space top view front view side view

What's your answer Teacher check

Problem of the week 78

Unit 2

A 1 27 2 46 3 191 4 353
5 122 6 438 7 665 8 61
9 54 10 389 11 540 12 207
13 472 14 736 15 134 16 473
17 825 18 459 19 870 20 738

B 1 142 2 215 3 873 4 529
5 604 6 919 7 450 8 738
9 175, 218, 715 10 97, 258, 301
11 487, 592, 903 12 599, 650, 711
13 182, 281, 812 14 791, 917, 971
15 203, 230, 302

C 1 F 2 T 3 F 4 T
5 T 6 F 7 F 8 T
9 F 10 T 11 T 12 T
13 F 14 F 15 T

Strategy
1 13 2 9 3 17 4 21
5 7 6 23 7 15 8 39
9 31

Follow directions the sun

Space cube, 6, 8, 12

Problem of the week 120

Unit 3

A 1 9 2 8 3 11 4 6
5 9 6 9 7 4 8 7
9 8 10 11 11 3 12 9
13 9 14 7 15 7 16 12
17 8 18 14 19 7 20 6

B 1 4 + 7 = 11 2 9 + 10 = 19
3 9 + 6 = 15 4 10 + 7 = 17
5 7 + 11 = 18 6 4 + 12 = 16
7 7 + 13 = 20 8 5 + 9 = 14
9 8 + 8 = 16 10 7 + 5 = 12
11 4 + 9 = 13 12 6 + 13 = 19
13 6 + 8 = 14 14 11 + 2 = 13
15 5 + 12 = 17

C 1 10 2 2 3 8 4 1
5 4th 6 9th 7 20 8 157
9 24 10 33 11 50 12 10
13 991 14 1999 15 Spring

Strategy
1 13 2 20 3 0 4 25
5 27 6 2 7 16 8 27
9 9 10 28 11 13 12 40

Space Teacher check

What's your question Teacher check

Problem of the week 50c, 10c, 10c, 10c, 10c, 5c, 5c, or 20c, 20c, 20c, 20c, 10c, 5c, 5c

Unit 4

A 1 60 2 8 3 70 4 15
5 40 6 14 7 10 8 10
9 16 10 10 11 12 12 20
13 35 14 50 15 25 16 45
17 18 18 30 19 40 20 100

Answers

B 1 18 2 30 3 eleven 4 19
5 102 6 100 7 81 8 36
9 158 10 161 11 25 12 28
13 499 14 203 15 70

C 1 teaspoon 2 milk jug
3 bath 4 thimble
5 drink 6 teacup
7 medicine glass 8 saucepan
9 newspaper 10 blanket
11 foot 12 poster
13 door mat 14 pizza
15 ruler

Strategy
1 18 2 17 3 19 4 14
5 16 6 18 7 29 8 27
9 25 10 43 11 38 12 36

Time
1 3:00 2 8:30 3 10:15 4 1:45

Space Teacher check

Problem of the week 3, 12, 21, 30, 102, 111, 120, 201, 210, 300

Unit 5

A 1 16 2 11 3 18 4 9
5 14 6 14 7 11 8 12
9 19 10 17 11 15 12 12
13 18 14 14 15 9 16 12
17 13 18 16 19 15 20 20

B 1 cm 2 m 3 m 4 cm
5 cm 6 m 7 cm 8 m
9-15 Teacher check

C 1 15, 19 2 9, 6
3 4, 8 4 6, 3
5 20, 29 6 41, 31
7 203, 303 8 25, 125
9 + 5 10 − 2
11 ÷ 2 12 + 10
13 × 10 14 × 2
15 − 9

Strategy
1 24 2 0 3 32 4 40
5 36 6 48 7 60 8 80
9 200 10 280

Fractions
1 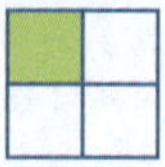 2  3  4 
5 circle 3 6 circle 5
7 circle 2 8 circle 3

Measurement ≈25 cm

Problem of the week
3, 10, 5, 2, 6, 7

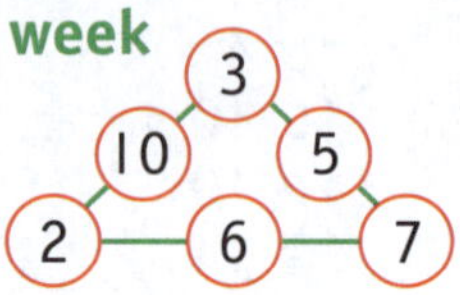

Unit 6

A 1 24 2 30 3 20 4 36
5 0 6 16 7 25 8 18
9 0 10 100 11 28 12 45
13 40 14 12 15 4 16 15
17 35 18 32 19 30 20 8

B 1  2  3  4 
5 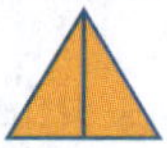 6 10 7 4 8 7
9 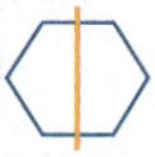 10 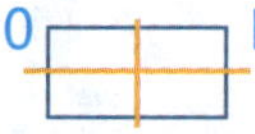 11 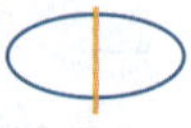 12 
13 25 14 10 15 12

C 1 24 2 18 3 24 4 35
5 32 6 25 7 16 8 0
9 50c 10 90c 11 75c 12 60c
13 15c 14 0 15 35c

Strategy
1 4, 40, 400 2 1, 10, 100
3 3, 30, 300 4 2, 20, 200
5 5, 50, 500 6 4, 40, 400

Fractions
1 $\frac{1}{5}$ 2 $\frac{1}{4}$ 3 $\frac{1}{6}$ 4 $\frac{1}{8}$
5 1 third 6 1 tenth
7 1 eighth 8 1 fifth

Problem of the week
1 blob 2 oil 3 hi 4 hole
5 lose 6 boss 7 glob 8 lie
9 goose 10 sole 11 hello 12 igloo
13 Teacher check

Unit 7

A
1 176 2 139 3 153 4 164
5 212 6 396 7 503 8 517
9 191 10 403 11 899 12 4
13 346 14 738 15 92 16 51
17 85 18 157 19 773 20 212

B
1 651 2 409 3 164 4 501
5 991 6 102 7 540 8 205
9 5 10 10 + 6 11 100 + 90 + 8
12 600 + 40 + 7 13 500 + 70 + 1
14 300 + 50 + 0 15 900 + 0 + 2

C
1 50c 2 80c 3 30c 4 85c
5 65c 6 5c 7 60c 8 35c
9 60c 10 95c 11 55c 12 90c
13 80c 14 $1 15 $1

Strategy
1 29 2 35 3 31 4 39
5 37 6 39 7 36 8 27
9 38 10 43

Time
1 1:15 2 6:35 3 11:00 4 4:50 5 9:20

Views Teacher check

Problem of the week 63

Unit 8

A
1 8 2 5 3 8 4 9
5 11 6 5 7 5 8 4
9 7 10 7 11 9 12 7
13 11 14 9 15 9 16 3
17 14 18 11 19 7 20 10

B
1 eighty-four
2 three hundred and sixteen
3 one hundred and twenty-eight
4 seven hundred and ten
5 five hundred and forty-two
6 eight hundred and eleven
7 nine hundred and ninety-nine
8 two hundred and four
9 six hundred and seventy
10 nineteen

C
1 60 2 30 3 15 4 45
5 120 6 24 7 7 8 12
9 Monday 10 Friday
11 Thursday 12 Saturday
13 14 14 January 15 December

Strategy
1 160 2 130 3 110 4 250
5 310 6 790 7 460 8 920
9 180 10 120 11 160 12 100
13 220 14 260 15 300

Space
1 cube
2 rectangular prism
3 triangular prism
4 hexagonal prism
5 pentagonal pyramid
6 square pyramid
7 triangular pyramid

Chance Teacher check

Problem of the week 8

Unit 9 - Revision

A
1 16 2 35 3 24 4 90
5 32 6 0 7 86 8 313
9 549 10 351 11 11 12 9
13 13 14 13 15 19 16 9
17 80 18 57 19 28 20 45

B
1 8 2 6 3 2 4 5
5 503 6 119 7 200
8 195, 203, 302 9 317 10 806
11 38 12 101 13 200 + 70 + 3
14 900 + 10 + 8 15 600 + 0 + 5

C
1 June 2 30 3 32 4 15
5 45c 6 90c 7 45 8 12
9 T 10 F 11 F 12 T
13 F 14 F 15 F

Strategy
1 50 2 39 3 31 4 19
5 23 6 3, 30, 300
7 9, 90, 900 8 60 9 88
10 730 11 560 12 460

Space Teacher check

Fraction
1 2 3 4

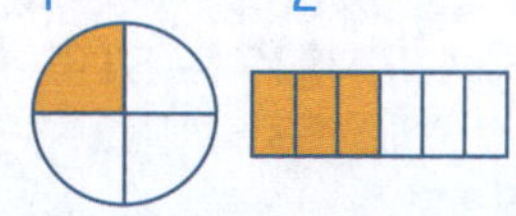

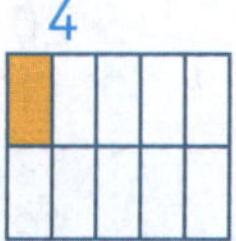

Answers

Time
1 9:20 2 12:40
Measurement Teacher check

Unit 10

A 1 20 2 20 3 19 4 19
5 19 6 19 7 17 8 7
9 9 10 12 11 17 12 2
13 14 14 15 15 9 16 8
17 7 18 7 19 7 20 6

B 1 7 2 30 3 400 4 1
5 50 6 8 7 600 8 0
9 83 10 228 11 541 12 719
13 307 14 912 15 670

C 1 $1.40 2 $12 3 25c 4 85c
5 60c 6 10 7 5 8 10
9 6 10 15 11 6 12 25c
13 4 14 4 15 10c

Strategy
1 13, 23 2 16, 26
3 7, 17 4 14, 24
5 12, 22 6 14, 24
7 11, 31 8 18, 48
9 11, 51

Abacus
1 246 2 417 3 335
4 506 5 840
6 – 10 Teacher check

Chance 1 1, 2, 3, 4, 5, 6 2 6
Space Triangular prism
Problem of the week NINE

Unit 11

A 1 4 2 11 3 9 4 3
5 8 6 9 7 8 8 3
9 7 10 7 11 8 12 6
13 5 14 7 15 8 16 6
17 5 18 7 19 8 20 11

B other answers possible
1 20 2 50 3 40 4 60
5 20 6 20 7 50 8 40
9 $17 + $23 10 $17 + $19
11 $23 + $19 12 $3 13 $31
14 $27 15 $85

C 1 square
2 triangle
3 pentagon
4 rectangle or square
5 hexagon
6 trapezium or triangle
7 triangle
8 octagon
9 triangular pyramids 10 cube
11 triangular prism
12 square pyramids

Strategy
1 3, 9, 6, 10, 7, 2
2 8, 5, 11, 9, 4, 7

Space
1 A sphere B cone C cylinder
2 & 3 Teachers check

Calculator Teachers check
Problem of the week Teacher check

Unit 12

A 1 7 2 12 3 7 4 13
5 16 6 7 7 18 8 11
9 16 10 5 11 4 12 19
13 8 14 19 15 10 16 14
17 19 18 6 19 12 20 19

B 1 257 2 964 3 832 4 695
5 164 6 373 7 508 8 920

C 1 $20 2 $1 3 $70 4 $1.80
5 $1 6 $4 7 $100 8 $300
9 24 10 4 11 19 12 19
13 22 14 12 15 50

Strategy
1 12 – 5 = 7, 7 + 5 = 12, 5 + 7 = 12
2 19 – 6 = 13, 6 + 13 =19, 13 + 6 = 19
3 15 – 7 = 8, 7 + 8 = 15, 8 + 7 = 15
4 9 + 7 = 16, 16 – 9 = 7, 16 – 7 = 9
5 7 + 6 = 13, 13 – 7 = 6, 13 – 6 = 7

Chance
1 I 2 I 3 C 4 L 5 L

Measurement Teacher check

Direction
1 A 2 A 3 H 4 Z
5 T 6 C 7 R 8 A

Problem of the week Answers will vary.
\$100 + \$50 + \$10 + \$10 + \$10 + \$10;
\$100 + \$50 + \$20 + \$10 + \$5 + \$5 etc

Unit 13

A 1 0 2 14 3 45 4 12
5 18 6 20 7 25 8 36
9 12 10 40 11 16 12 30
13 100 14 10 15 35 16 24
17 0 18 28 19 30 20 32

B 1 7 2 30 3 500 4 90
5 4 6 800 7 60 8 0
9 twenty-seven 10 forty-three
11 nineteen 12 seventy-eight
13 eleven 14 twelve
15 four hundred and six

C 1 1 month 2 1 m
3 2 min 4 1 year
5 5 tens 6 \$3 7 30 days
8 2 m 9 1 10 2 11 3
12 3 13 3 14 31 15 14

Strategy
1 65 2 170 ÷ 2 = 85
3 190 ÷ 2 = 95 4 140 ÷ 2 = 70
5 120 ÷ 2 = 60 6 180 ÷ 2 = 90
7 150 ÷ 2 = 75 8 220 ÷ 2 = 110

Hundredths Teacher check $\frac{1}{8}$.

Problem of the week Teacher check

Unit 14

A 1 22 2 13 3 18 4 19
5 19 6 22 7 19 8 18
9 21 10 23 11 22 12 22
13 24 14 19 15 19 16 17
17 17 18 23 19 19 20 23

B 1 \$1.10 2 60c 3 \$1 4 \$1.20
5 95c 6 \$1.10 7 \$1.55 8 \$1.85
9 \$1.65 10 \$2.20 11 \$2.35 12 \$2.40
13 \$3 14 \$3.15 15 \$4

C 1 10c 2 30c 3 95c 4 40c
5 75c 6 85c 7 40c 8 55c
9 \$1 10 \$2 11 \$3 12 \$3
13 \$9 14 \$5 15 \$9

Strategy
1 9 2 35 – 20 – 3 = 12
3 74 – 20 – 6 = 48 4 58 – 30 – 5 = 23
5 41 – 20 – 5 = 16 6 32 – 10 – 7 = 15
7 27 – 10 – 9 = 8 8 53 – 30 – 6 = 17

At the Fair
1a \$4 b \$6 2a \$2.60 b \$7.40
3a \$3.15 b \$6.85 4a \$3.45 b \$6.55
5a \$6.60 b \$3.40

Calculator
1 – 70 2 – 2000 3 – 50 4 – 500

Problem of the week
1 dollars 2 pounds 3 dong 4 baht
5 yen 6 rupiahs 7 rupees
8 ringgits

Unit 15

A 1 9 2 24 3 15
4 27 5 21 6 0
7 12 8 30 9 18
10 3 11 6

B 1 F 2 T
3 T 4 F
5 F 6 T
7 T 8 T

C 1 6 2 6 3 4 4 5
5 7 6 8 7 5 8 6
9 1:05 10 6:40 11 7:05 12 8:15
13 1:55 14 9:15 15 10:01

Strategy
1 48 2 120 3 60 4 100
5 88 6 200 7 160 8 84
9 168 10 240 11 64 12 56

Patterns
1 24, 4, 19 2 30, 6, 21
3 12, 0, 15 4 21, 3, 18
5 60, 16, 31 6 90, 26, 41
7 300, 96, 111 8 150, 46, 61

Capacity Teacher check

Problem of the week 2 horses, 2 spiders and 3 ducks

Answers

Unit 16

A 1 10 2 12 3 19 4 12
5 2 6 12 7 17 8 1
9 13 10 8 11 0 12 15
13 20 14 10 15 1 16 9
17 3 18 3 19 20 20 6

B 1 8 2 16 3 11 4 20
5 32 6 13 7 7000 8 16
9 $\frac{4}{5}$ 10 $\frac{4}{8}$ 11 $\frac{1}{5}$ 12 27
13 67 14 10

C 1 14 2 120 3 15 4 24
5 7 6 90 7 60 8 42
9 500 mL 10 100 mL
11 700 mL 12 300 mL
13 800 mL 14 400 mL
15 0 mL

Strategy
1 27 2 39 3 25 4 59
5 23 6 79 7 51 8 99
9 29 10 139 11 101 12 159
13 61 14 40 15 198

Time sequence Teacher check
Space Teacher check
Problem of the week 8 hrs and 35 mins

Unit 17

A 1 7 2 27 3 11 4 21
5 7 6 57 7 14 8 44
9 8 10 48 11 14 12 84
13 13 14 53 15 7 16 37
17 16 18 96 19 7 20 87

B 1 50c 2 20c 3 25c 4 75c
5 $1.20 6 $1.85 7 $1.05 8 0.65c
9 $\frac{3}{10}$ 10 $\frac{5}{6}$ 11 $\frac{4}{8}$ 12 $\frac{3}{5}$
13 $\frac{3}{4}$ 14 $\frac{1}{4}$ 15 $\frac{1}{2}$

C 1 5 2 3 3 8 4 7
5 4 6 6 7 8 8 5
9 35 10 98 11 4 12 $1
13 12 14 88 15 32

Strategy
1 70 2 300 3 840 4 1500
5 1630 6 2600 7 110 8 900
9 3100 10 940 11 8500 12 180
13 9000 14 30 400 15 800

Data
1 Joy 2 Jill and John
3 Jim 4 28 5 Jan

Space Teacher check
Problem of the week 5

Unit 18

A 1 19 2 17 3 7 4 11
5 7 6 24 7 24 8 6
9 15 10 13 11 0 12 18
13 10 14 27 15 40 16 8
17 38 18 0 19 21 20 90

B 1 700 2 700 + 20 + 8 3 293
4 30 5 $13 6 $65
7 thirty-seven
8 nine hundred and four 9 22
10 $\frac{4}{4}$ or 1 11 6 12 false 13 false
14 F 15 T

C 1 $24 2 6
3 9 4 square
5 pentagon 6 hexagon
7 $1 8 $350
9 19 10 14
11 2 12 30 13 8:35 14 3:01
15 700 mL

Strategy
1 16, 36 2 13, 63 3 83 4 97
5 75 6 95 7 64 8 160
9 51 10 79 11 190 12 4100
13 700 14 600 15 5 16 5

Abacus
1 216 2

Space
1 cone
2

Chance
1 head or tail 2 2
3 head + head, tail + tail, head + tail

Patterns
1 17, 48 2 24, 60

Unit 19

A
1 15 2 10 3 27 4 12
5 21 6 11 7 12 8 25
9 23 10 13 11 24 12 24
13 23 14 22 15 24 16 18
17 24 18 23 19 12 20 16

B
1 600 + 40 + 3 2 200 + 10 + 9
3 452 4 500 5 80 6 0
7 199 8 90 9 $1.31 10 $1.51
11 $1.44 12 $1.38 13 $1.23 14 $1.59
15 $1.96

C
1 rockmelon 2 television
3 shoe 4 mobile phone
5 pencil 6 pumpkin
7 sandwich 8 coat
9 am 10 pm 11 pm 12 am
13 pm 14 am 15 am

Strategy
1 67 2 95 3 45
4 64 + 3 – 2 = 92
5 35 + 40 – 2 = 73
6 79 + 20 – 1 = 98
7 43 + 40 – 1 = 82
8 18 + 70 – 2 = 86

Data
1 Jen 2 Jim 3 $5 4 $19
5 $25 6 $44

Problem of the week

16	2	12
6	10	14
8	18	4

Unit 20

A
1 18 2 54 3 12 4 30
5 42 6 48 7 6 8 60
9 24 10 36 11 0 12 9
13 72 14 45 15 36 16 63
17 18 18 27 19 90 20 54

B
1 12 2 3 × 5 = 15
3 3 × 7 = 21 4 4 × 8 = 32
5 2 × 5 = 10 6 4 × 4 = 16
7 3 × 3 = 9 8 5 × 10 = 50
9 6 × 9 = 54 10 5 × 4 = 20
11 6 × 6 = 36 12 4 × 0 = 0
13 6 × 7 = 42 14 9 × 7 = 63

C
1 20c + 10c + 5c 2 50c + 20c + 10c
3 $1 + 20c + 20c 4 50c + 20c + 20c
5 $2 + 10c + 5c 6 $1+50c+20c+5c
7 $2 + 50c + 10c 8 $2+$2+20c+5c
9 $50 + $10 10 $50 + $20 + $10
11 $10 + $5 12 $20 + $20 + $5
13 $50 + $20 + $20 14 $50 + $20 + $5
15 $100 + $10 + $5

Strategy
1 81 2 29 + 30 + 4 = 63
3 18 + 40 + 3 = 61 4 57 + 30 + 6 = 93
5 62 + 10 + 9 = 81 6 45 + 30 + 8 = 83
7 16 + 50 + 8 = 74 8 21 + 70 + 7 = 98

Multiplication
1 21 2 36 3 56 4 36 5 72

Space Teacher check

Problem of the week
Toddy – he ate 40 per hour

Unit 21

A
1 16 2 0 3 36 4 28
5 81 6 36 7 15 8 25
9 72 10 32 11 0 12 42
13 24 14 35 15 48 16 63
17 50 18 0 19 54 20 24

B
1 10 2 9 3 8 4 6
5 6 6 6 7 24 8 6
9 3 months 10 5 years
11 10 years 12 3
13 $2 14 50 cm 15 200 mL

C
1 $\frac{1}{2}$ 2 $\frac{1}{2}$ 3 $\frac{3}{4}$ 4 $\frac{2}{8}$
5 $\frac{2}{5}$ 6 $\frac{3}{8}$ 7 $\frac{3}{5}$ 8 $\frac{4}{5}$
9 $>$ 10 = 11 $<$ 12 $>$
13 $>$ 14 = 15 $>$

Strategy
1 17, 7 2 26, 16 3 48, 38
4 54, 44 5 25, 15 6 31, 21
7 67, 57 8 47, 37

Fractions Teacher check

Problem of the week 68, 73, 76, 81, 86, 87, 92, 94, 99, 105

Answers

Unit 22

A
1 12 | 2 9 | 3 6 | 4 4
5 6 | 6 3 | 7 7 | 8 5
9 7 | 10 7 | 11 9 | 12 8
13 5 | 14 10 | 15 4 | 16 3
17 8 | 18 6 | 19 10 | 20 24

B
1 28 | 2 45 | 3 42 | 4 48
5 16 | 6 54 | 7 21 | 8 32
9 5 | 10 6 | 11 4 | 12 4
13 6 | 14 9

C
1 7 | 2 13 | 3 8 | 4 30
5 9 | 6 9 | 7 10 | 8 17
9 2 | 10 mL | 11 $\frac{1}{2}$ | 12 250 mL
13 150 | 14 30 | 15 $\frac{1}{4}$

Strategy
1 60 + 30 + 4 + 7 = 101
2 30 + 20 + 6 + 9 = 65
3 10 + 70 + 7 + 7 = 94
4 50 + 30 + 3 + 7 = 90
5 20 + 60 + 5 + 5 = 90
6 40 + 40 + 9 + 2 = 91
7 70 + 10 + 8 + 5 = 93
8 80 + 20 + 5 + 4 = 109

Fair shares
1 9 | 2 6 | 3 18 | 4 3
5 2 | 6 4 | 7 1 | 8 12

Measurement Teacher check

Problem of the week
1 2 + 3 + 4 | 2 3 + 4 + 5 + 6
3 7 + 8 + 9 | 4 8 + 9 + 10 + 11

Unit 23

A
1 8 | 2 16 | 3 10 | 4 15
5 12 | 6 19 | 7 8 | 8 12
9 12 | 10 15 | 11 17 | 12 15
13 18 | 14 11 | 15 6 | 16 18
17 17 | 18 9 | 19 18 | 20 9

B
1 8 | 2 18 | 3 40 | 4 16
5 20 | 6 5 | 7 45 | 8 20
9 14 | 10 45 | 11 1000 | 12 $\frac{1}{4}$
13 78 | 14 67 | 15 12

C
1 4 | 2 20 | 3 20 | 4 0
5 62c | 6 42c | 7 50 | 8 500
9 60 | 10 30 | 11 $2.50 | 12 365/6
13 24 | 14 33 | 15 12

Strategy
1 48 | 2 16 | 3 40 | 4 72
5 160 | 6 32 | 7 64 | 8 240
9 96 | 10 200 | 11 0 | 12 800
13 88 | 14 168 | 15 120

Calculator Puzzle Teacher check

Problem of the week
4, 5, 9; 3, 4, 5; 5, 9, 10; 9, 10, 11
Sum: 18, 12, 24, 30

Unit 24

A
1 36 | 2 9 | 3 72 | 4 8
5 42 | 6 8 | 7 25 | 8 0
9 56 | 10 8 | 11 48 | 12 1
13 36 | 14 64 | 15 35 | 16 9
17 27 | 18 3 | 19 49 | 20 9

B
1 T | 2 F | 3 T | 4 T
5 F | 6 F | 7 T | 8 F
9 T | 10 T | 11 F | 12 T
13 F | 14 F | 15 T

C
1 I | 2 C | 3 P | 4 P
5 P | 6 C | 7 I | 8 P
9 – 11 Teacher check

Strategy
1 4 x 3 x 2 = 24
2 5 x 3 x 2 = 30
3 6 x 3 x 2 = 36
4 7 x 3 x 2 = 42
5 8 x 3 x 2 = 48
6 9 x 3 x 2 = 54

Number Muncher
1 29 | 2 35 | 3 38 | 4 68
5 308

Patterns
1 Teacher check | 2 21 | 3 33

Problem of the week 1925

Unit 25

A 1 8 2 13 3 8 4 7
5 11 6 7 7 13 8 16
9 9 10 16 11 3 12 20
13 20 14 20 15 18 16 14
17 0 18 14 19 13 20 2

B 1 b 2 d 3 a 4 c
5 f 6 g 7 h 8 e
9 < 10 = 11 > 12 <
13 > 14 > 15 <

C 1 apple 2 chair 3 horse
4 baby 5 bus 6 bicycle
7 shoe 8 pencil case
9 cm 10 mL 11 mm
12 L 13 kg 14 m 15 g

Strategy
1 60 2 80 3 90 4 100
5 65 6 95 7 85 8 75
9 150 10 125 11 140 12 115

Symmetry Teacher check

Mass
1 BAC 2A 4000 g B 2500 g C 7000 g

Problem of the week 80 L

Unit 26

A 1 27 2 26 3 27 4 29
5 31 6 24 7 28 8 32
9 30 10 28 11 33 12 28
13 28 14 29 15 27 16 30
17 31 18 29 19 37 20 37

B 1 c 2 a 3 d 4 b
5 f 6 h 7 e 8 g
9 k 10 i 11 l 12 j
13 o 14 n 15 m

C 1 F 2 F 3 T 4 T
5 T 6 T 7 F 8 F
9 F 10 T 11 F 12 T
13 F 14 F 15 T/F

Strategy
1 35 2 60 3 56 4 52
5 58 6 64 7 37 8 73
9 78 10 54 11 57 12 63
13 41 14 67 15 52

Measurement
1a 44 mm b 40 mm c 25 mm d 67 mm
2 Teacher check

Space 3D 1 triangular pyramid 2 cylinder or sphere

Problem of the week 1 × 48, 2 × 24, 3 × 16, 4 × 12, 6 × 8, 8 × 6, 12 × 4, 16 × 3, 24 × 2, 48 × 1

Unit 27 – Revision

A 1 72 2 21 3 30 4 16
5 54 6 8 7 12 8 32
9 10 10 16 11 3 12 0
13 10 14 29 15 8 16 12
17 42 18 27 19 36 20 4

B 1 9 2 23 3 36 4 2
5 $1.30 6 9 7 24 8 $1.15
9 2 10 $45 11 $2.55 12 20
13 5 14 27 15 40

C 1 8 2 42c 3 48 4 85c
5 4 6 5-6 cm 7 13 8 $\frac{4}{8}$
9 $2 10 4 11 2000 12 180
13 350 14 $2.50 15 5·5

Strategy
1 91 2 71 3 73 4 38
5 18 6 64 7 96 8 56
9 95 10 150 11 270 12 32, 42

Space Teacher check

Fractions Teacher check

Measurement 1 35 mm 2 53 mm
3 & 4 Teacher check

Money 1 $23.50 2 $6.50

Unit 28

A 1 17 2 12 3 17 4 15
5 22 6 17 7 20 8 22
9 15 10 21 11 19 12 21
13 24 14 19 15 22 16 19
17 19 18 22 19 14 20 21

B 1 70 2 30 3 50 4 90
5 50 6 60 7 20 8 30
9 500 10 600 11 500 12 500
13 600 14 500 15 600

Answers

C 1 = 2 > 3 > 4 <
5 = 6 < 7 > 8 >
9 20 10 36 11 10 12 30
13 52 14 120 15 2000

Strategy
1 43 + 10 + 5 = 58 2 43 – 10 – 5 = 28
3 38 + 20 + 6 = 64 4 38 – 20 – 6 = 12
5 34 + 20 + 7 = 61 6 34 – 20 – 7 = 7
7 54 + 20 + 9 = 83 8 54 – 20 – 9 = 25

Number
1 Teacher check 2A 1050 B 1950
C 1400 D 1150 E 1630

Problem of the week 96

Unit 29

A 1 14 2 70 3 0 4 42
5 28 6 21 7 70 8 49
9 56 10 14 11 28 12 63
13 35 14 0 15 7 16 42
17 56 18 35 19 21 20 63

B 1 42, 28, 70, 63, 49, 35, 56
2 64, 48, 24, 72, 32, 56

C 1 8 2 30 3 20 4 5
5 20 6 15 7 11 8 200
9 21 10 30 11 14 12 23
13 40 14 6 15 54

Strategy
1 3 x 3 x 3 = 27 2 5 x 3 x 3 = 45
3 6 x 3 x 3 = 54 4 7 x 3 x 3 = 63
5 8 x 3 x 3 = 72 6 9 x 3 x 3 = 81

Multiplication
1 × 36, 2 × 18, 3 × 12, 4 × 9, 6 × 6, 9 × 4, 12 × 3, 18 × 2, 36 × 1

Time
1 Tuesday 2 9th 3 4
4 Wednesday 5 Sunday

Problem of the week
= 3 = 2 = 5 = 1 = 4

Unit 30

A 1 5 2 6 3 6 4 7
5 10 6 2 7 1 8 7
9 9 10 10 11 4 12 0
13 11 14 22 15 3 16 2
17 3 18 17 19 7 20 6

B 1 4 × 7 = 28 2 6 × 6 = 36
3 8 × 9 = 72 4 9 × 5 = 45
5 7 × 7 = 49 6 9 × 9 = 81
7 5 × 7 = 35 8 6 × 7 = 42
9 9 10 10 11 8 12 8
13 8 14 11 15 7

C 1 100 2 10 3 1000 4 15
5 24 6 45 7 6 8 31
9 56 10 49 11 120 12 100
13 20 14 10 15 500

Strategy
1 5 2 7 3 7 4 7
5 7 6 7 7 6 8 3
9 8 10 4 11 6 12 6

Calculator
1 5040 2 3360 mm 3 13 000

Time
1 twenty to seven 2 five past three
3 five to one
4 quarter to twelve

Problem of the week 10

Unit 31

A 1 6 2 10 3 2 4 6
5 8 6 1 7 9 8 7
9 2 10 4 11 8 12 9
13 4 14 1 15 3 16 10
17 7 18 3 19 5 20 5

B 1 5 2 3 3 8
4 4 = 4 5 8 = 2
6 2 = 10 7 20 ÷ 4 = 5
8 20 ÷ 5 = 4 9 20 ÷ 10 = 2
10 24 ÷ 2 = 12 11 24 ÷ 4 = 6
12 24 ÷ 3 = 8

C 1 T 2 F 3 F 4 T
5 F 6 T 7 T 8 T
9 circular 10 sphere 11 cylinder
12 6 13 6 14 5 15 rectangle

Strategy

1 $8 \times 7 = 56$, $56 \div 8 = 7$, $56 \div 7 = 8$
2 $4 \times 9 = 36$, $36 \div 9 = 4$, $36 \div 4 = 9$
3 $9 \times 6 = 54$, $54 \div 6 = 9$, $54 \div 9 = 6$
4 $48 \div 8 = 6$, $8 \times 6 = 48$, $6 \times 8 = 48$
5 $63 \div 9 = 7$, $9 \times 7 = 63$, $7 \times 9 = 63$

Space Teacher check
Fractions Teacher check
Problem of the week

Is it odd?
- Yes: 15, 21, 31, 23
  - Is it a multiple of 3?
    - Yes: 15, 21
    - No: 31, 23
- No: 24, 34, 42, 16
  - Is it a multiple of 4?
    - Yes: 24, 16
    - No: 34, 42

Unit 32

A

1 10	2 7	3 19	4 9
5 21	6 16	7 9	8 12
9 7	10 7	11 12	12 16
13 20	14 15	15 20	16 8
17 14	18 17	19 0	20 17

B

1 2	2 7	3 9	4 $4\frac{1}{2}$
5 300	6 650	7 2	8 8
9 30	10 70	11 100	12 15
13 17	14 142	15 503	

C

1 36	2 28	3 60	4 28
5 $3.15	6 $2.80	7 Teacher check	
8 18 cm	9 5	10 8	11 180
12 30	13 $1.05	14 Teacher check	
15 20c			

Strategy

1 104	2 75	3 84	4 68
5 54	6 84	7 117	8 114

Area 1 a 9 b 12
2 Teacher check
Chance Teacher check
Problem of the week 1 + 2 + 34 + 56 + 7

Unit 33

A

1 21	2 81	3 48	4 25
5 0	6 24	7 80	8 24
9 63	10 54	11 42	12 72
13 32	14 36	15 100	16 45
17 40	18 63	19 0	20 18

B

1 卌|| 2 卌|||| 3 卌卌|
4 卌卌卌||
5 卌卌卌卌卌||||
6 卌卌|||
7 卌卌卌卌卌卌||||
8 卌卌卌卌卌卌卌卌卌| 9 8

10 12	11 15	12 31	13 24
14 19	15 40		

C

1 square	2 circle
3 octagon	4 hexagon
5 trapezium	6 right angle
7 pentagon	8 parallelogram
9 cone	10 prism
11 cylinder	12 pyramid
13 cube 14 sphere	15 square prism

Strategy

1 240	2 180	3 270	4 90
5 60	6 150	7 120	8 300
9 330	10 600		

Space Teacher check
Position I AM A MATHS WIZ
Problem of the week Teacher check

Unit 34

A

1 27	2 9	3 42	4 5
5 63	6 7	7 81	8 1
9 32	10 8	11 64	12 4
13 49	14 10	15 30	16 8
17 0	18 9	19 9	20 7

B

1 12	2 18	3 18	4 18
5 4	6 32	7 9	8 160
9 12	10 5	11 27	12 35
13 21	14 4	15 30	

C

1 T	2 F	3 F	4 T
5 T	6 F	7 T	8 F
9 F	10 T	11 F	12 F
13 T	14 T	15 F	

Answers

Strategy

1 22	2 21	3 26	4 19
5 18	6 31	7 28	8 37
9 28	10 33	11 29	12 41

Position

1 D4 2 B3 3 C2 4 B1
5 circle

Direction

1 left 2 above 3 below 4 right

Problem of the week

Kylie, Charlie, Amanda, Barry, Sal or vice versa

Unit 35 – Revision

A

1 20	2 0	3 11	4 13
5 42	6 4	7 7	8 8
9 30	10 7	11 10	12 21
13 9	14 4	15 9	16 11
17 64	18 100	19 24	20 1

B

1 70	2 200	3 2	4 ÷
5 7	6 4	7 $\frac{5}{10}$	8 12
9 21	10 0	11 9	12 F
13 $\frac{1}{2}$	14 23	15 F	

C

1 20	2 10	3 20	4 16
5 9	6 6	7 4	
8 Tuesday		9 L	10 24
11 56	12 $7.25	13 80	14 500
15 December			

Strategy

1 59	2 29	3 370	4 800
5 3600	6 5	7 45	8 80
9 63	10 9	11 9	12 63

Number Teacher check

Space Teacher check

Time 1 ten to six 2 five past twelve

Position

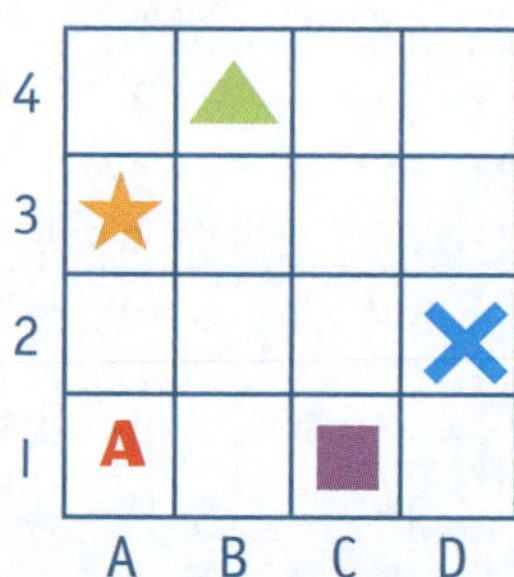

Unit 17

Strategy
Multiply by 10
Multiply by 100

×10 – add a zero eg 9 × 10 = 90, 18 × 10 = 180

×100 – add two zeros eg 6 × 100 = 600, 27 × 100 = 2 700

1 7 × 10 = ______
2 3 × 100 = ______
3 84 × 10 = ______
4 15 × 100 = ______
5 163 × 10 = ______
6 26 × 100 = ______
7 11 × 10 = ______
8 9 × 100 = ______
9 31 × 100 = ______
10 94 × 10 = ______
11 85 × 100 = ______
12 18 × 10 = ______
13 90 × 100 = ______
14 304 × 100 = ______
15 80 × 10 = ______

Score

Data

1 Who ate the most? ______

2 Who ate the same number of pieces? ______

3 Who did not like fruit? ______

4 How many pieces were eaten altogether? ______

5 Who do you think ate 1 piece every day? ______

Score

Space

Draw:

1 parallel lines.

2 a trapezium.

Problem of the week

Jacqui rated days as Great, OK, Rather Forget or Dreadful.

In June she said there were 10 Great days and the same number of Rather Forget days.

If there were equal numbers of OK and Dreadful days how many days were OK?

Unit 18 Revision

A

1 5 + 14 = ______
2 9 + 8 = ______
3 20 − 13 = ______
4 20 − 9 = ______
5 19 − 12 = ______
6 17 + 7 = ______
7 19 + 5 = ______
8 7 + 8 − 9 = ______
9 8 − 5 + 12 = ______
10 15 − 11 + 9 = ______
11 7 × 0 = ______
12 6 × 3 = ______
13 5 + 12 − 7 = ______
14 9 × 3 = ______
15 5 × 8 = ______
16 17 − 9 = ______
17 47 − 9 = ______
18 384 × 0 = ______
19 16 + 5 = ______
20 85 + 5 = ______

Score

B

1 Value of 7 in 3 715? ______
2 728 = ______ + ______ + ______
3 ______ = 200 + 90 + 3
4 Estimate only. 67 − 41 = ______
5 $20 − $7 = ______
6 $100 − $35 = ______

Write in words.

7 37 ______
8 904 ______

Write the next number.

9 7, 12, 17, ______
10 $\frac{1}{4}$, $\frac{2}{4}$, $\frac{3}{4}$, ______
11 48, 24, 12, ______

True or false?

12 16 + 21 = 47 ______
13 98 − 98 = 1 ______
14 $\frac{6}{10} = \frac{1}{2}$ ______
15 $\frac{3}{3} = 1$ ______

Score

C

1 4 cakes at $6 each? ______
2 $\frac{1}{2}$ a dozen = ______
3 $\frac{1}{5}$ of 45 apples = ______

What 2D shape has:

4 4 equal sides? ______
5 5 angles? ______
6 6 sides? ______
7 5 lots of 20c = ______
8 7 lots of $50 = ______
9 sum of 8 and 11 ______
10 difference between 17 and 3 ______
11 days in 48 hours ______
12 days in June ______
13 time 5 min before 8:40 ______
14 time 1 min after 3 o'clock ______
15 300 mL + ______ = 1 L

Score

Revision

Strategy

Use the strategies you have learnt.

1 9 + 7 = ______

29 + 7 = ______

2 8 + 5 = ______

58 + 5 = ______

3 64 + 19 = ______

4 75 + 22 = ______

5 15 × 5 = ______

6 19 × 5 = ______

7 16 × 4 = ______

8 40 × 4 = ______

9 26 + 25 = ______

10 40 + 39 = ______

11 19 × 10 = ______

12 41 × 100 = ______

13 70 × 10 = ______

14 30 × 20 = ______

15 53 − 48 = ______

16 91 − 86 = ______

Score

Abacus

1 What is the number?

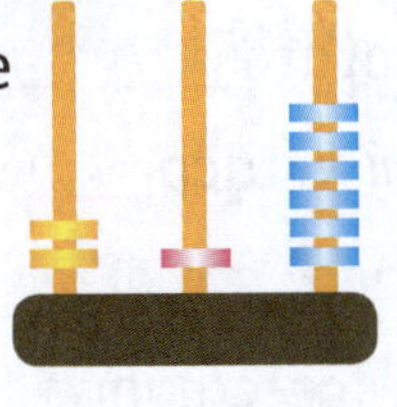

2 Draw 604.

Space

1 Name the object. ______

2 Draw the views from:

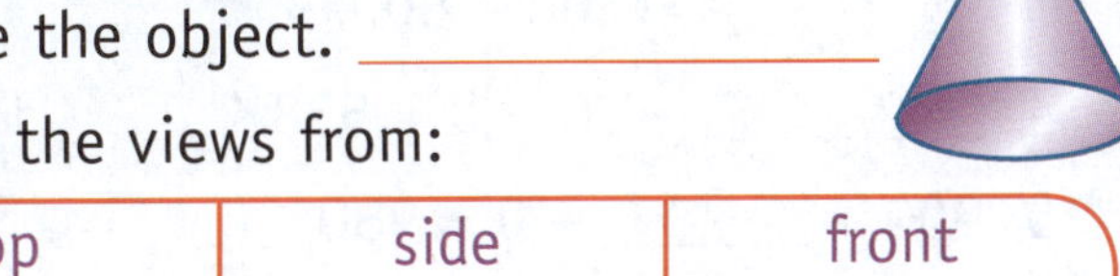

top	side	front

Chance

You toss a 20c coin.

1 What outcomes can you toss?

______

2 How many outcomes are there?

______

3 What outcomes can you toss if you use two 20c coins?

______

Patterns

Here are two Number Changing Factories.

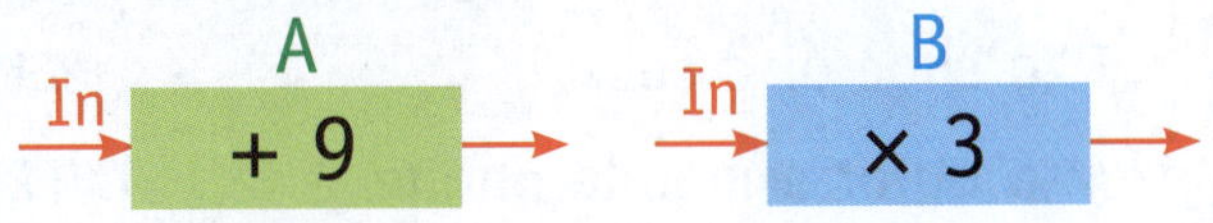

What do these numbers become in each factory?

	Number	A	B
1	8		
2	20		

Unit 19

A

1 8 + 7 = ______

2 7 + 3 = ______

3 19 + 8 = ______

4 6 + 6 = ______

5 18 + 3 = ______

6 7 + 4 = ______

7 9 + 3 = ______

8 19 + 6 = ______

9 16 + 7 = ______

10 8 + 5 = ______

11 17 + 7 = ______

12 16 + 8 = ______

13 19 + 4 = ______

14 17 + 5 = ______

15 18 + 6 = ______

16 14 + 4 = ______

17 19 + 5 = ______

18 17 + 6 = ______

19 8 + 4 = ______

20 9 + 7 = ______

Score

B

1 643 = ______ + ______ + ______

2 219 = ______ + ______ + ______

3 ______ = 400 + 50 + 2

4 ______ + 30 + 8 = 538

5 900 + ______ + 0 = 980

6 703 = 700 + ______ + 3

7 100 + 90 + 9 = ______

8 300 + ______ + 7 = 397

9 cake + ice-cream ______

10 potato + taco ______

11 cake + potato ______

12 ice-cream + taco ______

13 cake + taco ______

14 potato + ice-cream ______

15 cake + taco + ice-cream ______

73c

58c

86c

65c

Score

C Circle the one that weighs more.

1 an apple or a rockmelon

2 a book or a television

3 a shoe or a sock

4 a CD or a mobile phone

5 a feather or a pencil

6 a lemon or a pumpkin

7 a sandwich or a biscuit

8 a coat or a scarf

am or pm?

9 Breakfast is at 7:50 ______.

10 Sunset was at 6:29 ______.

11 Jy ate lunch at 12:08 ______.

12 School started at 9:15 ______.

13 The postman came at 3:42 ______.

14 Maths started at 11:25 ______.

15 The alarm rang at 6:05 ______.

Score

Strategy
Compensation strategy

42 + 29 = 42 + 30 − 1
(= 72 − 1)
= 71

1 38 + 29 = 38 + 30 − 1
= ______

2 56 + 39 = 56 + 40 − 1
= ______

3 27 + 18 = 27 + 20 − 2
= ______

4 64 + 28 = ______
= ______

5 35 + 38 = ______
= ______

6 79 + 19 = ______
= ______

7 43 + 39 = ______
= ______

8 18 + 68 = ______
= ______

Score

Data

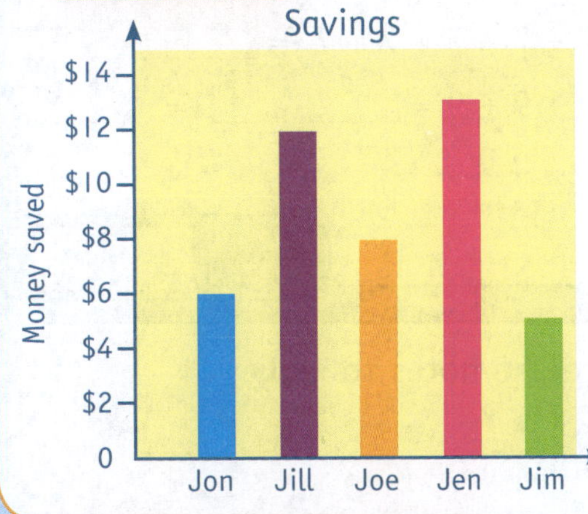

1 Who saved the most? ______

2 Who saved the least? ______

3 How much did Jim save? ______

4 How much did the boys save? ______

5 How much did the girls save? ______

6 How much did the children save altogether? ______

Score

Problem of the week

Complete this magic square so each row, column and diagonal adds to 30.

16	2	
8		

Unit 20

A

1 $6 \times 3 =$ ______
2 $6 \times 9 =$ ______
3 $2 \times 6 =$ ______
4 $6 \times 6 =$ ______
5 $5 \times 6 =$ ______
6 $6 \times 7 =$ ______
7 $8 \times 6 =$ ______
8 $6 \times 1 =$ ______
9 $10 \times 6 =$ ______
10 $4 \times 6 =$ ______
11 $9 \times 0 =$ ______
12 $1 \times 9 =$ ______
13 $9 \times 8 =$ ______
14 $9 \times 5 =$ ______
15 $9 \times 4 =$ ______
16 $7 \times 9 =$ ______
17 $9 \times 2 =$ ______
18 $3 \times 9 =$ ______
19 $9 \times 10 =$ ______
20 $9 \times 6 =$ ______

Score

Write as multiplication.

B

1 $3 + 3 + 3 + 3 =$ 4 x 3 = ______
2 $5 + 5 + 5 =$ ______ = ______
3 $7 + 7 + 7 =$ ______ = ______
4 $8 + 8 + 8 + 8 =$ ______ = ______
5 $5 + 5 =$ ______ = ______
6 $4 + 4 + 4 + 4 =$ ______ = ______
7 $3 + 3 + 3 =$ ______ = ______
8 $10 + 10 + 10 + 10 + 10 =$ ______ = ______
9 $9 + 9 + 9 + 9 + 9 + 9 =$ ______ = ______
10 $4 + 4 + 4 + 4 + 4 =$ ______ = ______
11 $6 + 6 + 6 + 6 + 6 + 6 =$ ______ = ______
12 $0 + 0 + 0 + 0 =$ ______ = ______
13 $7 + 7 + 7 + 7 + 7 + 7 =$ ______ = ______
14 $9 + 9 + 9 + 9 =$ ______ = ______

Score

Write the least number of coins to make:

C

1 35c 20c + 10c + ______
2 80c ______
3 $1.40 ______
4 90c ______
5 $2.15 ______
6 $1.75 ______
7 $2.60 ______
8 $4.25 ______

Write the notes to make:

9 $60 ______
10 $80 ______
11 $15 ______
12 $45 ______
13 $90 ______
14 $75 ______
15 $115 ______

Score

Strategy

Jump strategy for addition

26 + 35 = 26 + 30 + 5
= 56 + 5
= 61

1 35 + 46 = 35 + 40 + 6
= ______

2 29 + 34 = ______
= ______

3 18 + 43 = ______
= ______

4 57 + 36 = ______
= ______

5 62 + 19 = ______
= ______

6 45 + 38 = ______
= ______

7 16 + 58 = ______
= ______

8 21 + 77 = ______
= ______

Score

Multiplication

1 3 birds' nests with 7 baby birds in each. How many baby birds? ______

2 9 horses. How many legs? ______

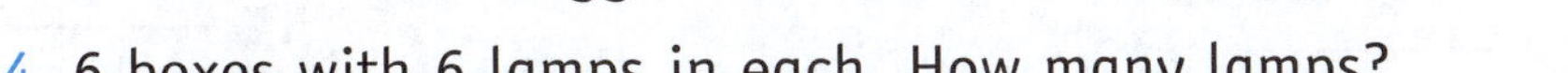

3 7 baskets with 8 eggs in each. How many eggs? ______

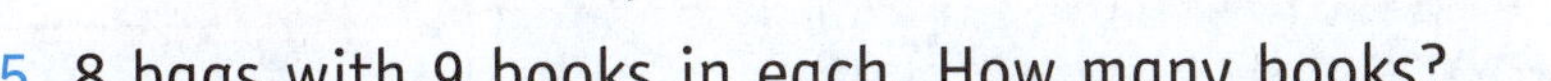

4 6 boxes with 6 lamps in each. How many lamps? ______

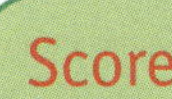

5 8 bags with 9 books in each. How many books? ______

Score

Space

Colour the trapeziums.

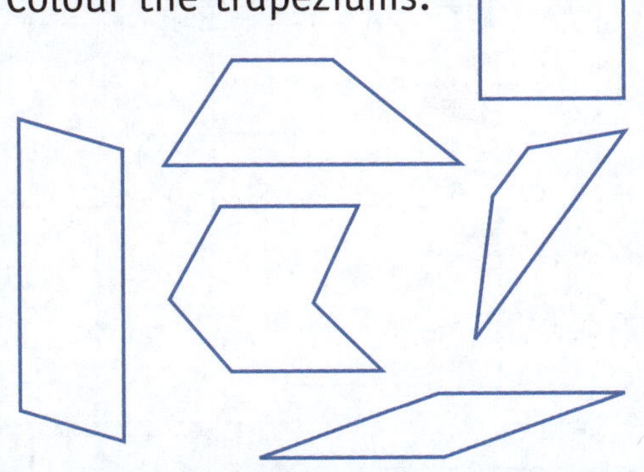

Problem of the week

Toddy and Tilly were arguing over who was the slowest eater. "I eat only 100 baked beans in $2\frac{1}{2}$ hours," said Toddy. "Well I eat only 168 in 4 hours," said Tilly.

Who was the slowest eater? ______

How do you know?

______

______

Unit 21

A

1. 4 × 4 = ______
2. 0 × 6 = ______
3. 6 × 6 = ______
4. 4 × 7 = ______
5. 9 × 9 = ______
6. 4 × 9 = ______
7. 5 × 3 = ______
8. 5 × 5 = ______
9. 9 × 8 = ______
10. 4 × 8 = ______
11. 0 × 9 = ______
12. 6 × 7 = ______
13. 3 × 8 = ______
14. 5 × 7 = ______
15. 6 × 8 = ______
16. 9 × 7 = ______
17. 5 × 10 = ______
18. 3 × 0 = ______
19. 9 × 6 = ______
20. 6 × 4 = ______

Score

B

1. half of 20 ______
2. quarter of 36 ______
3. one fifth of 40 ______
4. one eighth of 48 ______
5. quarter of 24 ______
6. one tenth of 60 ______
7. half of 48 ______
8. one fifth of 30 ______
9. quarter of 1 year ______
10. half of 1 decade ______
11. one tenth of 1 century ______
12. quarter of 1 dozen ______
13. one fifth of $10 ______
14. half of 1 metre ______
15. one fifth of 1 litre ______

Score

C

Circle the larger fraction.

1. $\frac{1}{2}$ $\frac{1}{5}$
2. $\frac{1}{4}$ $\frac{1}{2}$
3. $\frac{3}{4}$ $\frac{3}{8}$
4. $\frac{2}{8}$ $\frac{1}{10}$
5. $\frac{2}{5}$ $\frac{2}{10}$
6. $\frac{1}{4}$ $\frac{3}{8}$
7. $\frac{1}{2}$ $\frac{3}{5}$
8. $\frac{4}{5}$ $\frac{6}{10}$

Use <, > or =.

9. $\frac{1}{2}$ ______ $\frac{1}{4}$
10. $\frac{1}{2}$ ______ $\frac{5}{10}$
11. $\frac{1}{5}$ ______ $\frac{5}{10}$
12. $\frac{3}{4}$ ______ $\frac{1}{2}$
13. $\frac{1}{4}$ ______ $\frac{1}{10}$
14. $\frac{2}{4}$ ______ $\frac{5}{10}$
15. $\frac{3}{5}$ ______ $\frac{4}{10}$

Write the fraction.

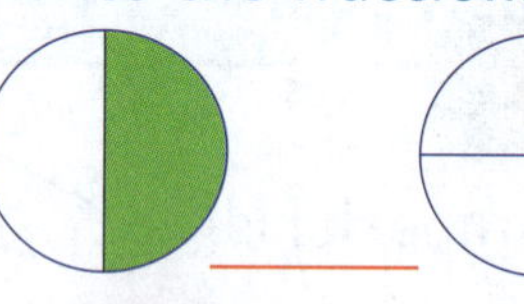
______ ______

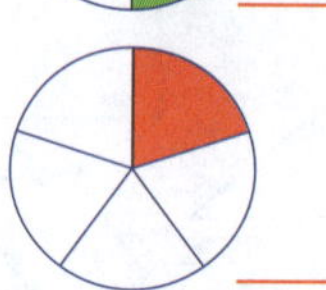
______

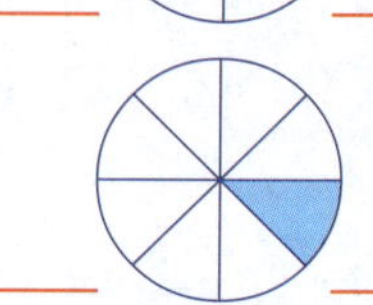
______

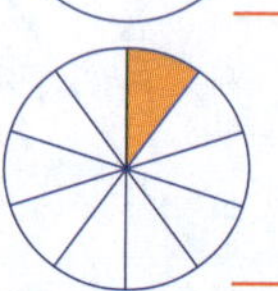
______

Score

Unit 21

Strategy
Find the pattern

eg 60 − 3 = 57
60 − 13 = 47

82 − 4 = 78
82 − 14 = 68

1 21 − 4 = ______
21 − 14 = ______

2 35 − 9 = ______
35 − 19 = ______

3 56 − 8 = ______
56 − 18 = ______

4 62 − 8 = ______
62 − 18 = ______

5 34 − 9 = ______
34 − 19 = ______

6 38 − 7 = ______
38 − 17 = ______

7 74 − 7 = ______
74 − 17 = ______

8 55 − 8 = ______
55 − 18 = ______

Score

Fractions
Colour the fraction.

1 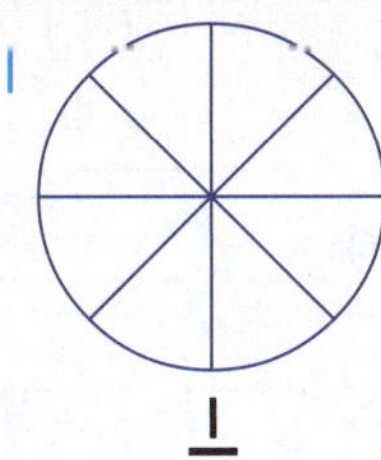
$\frac{1}{2}$

2 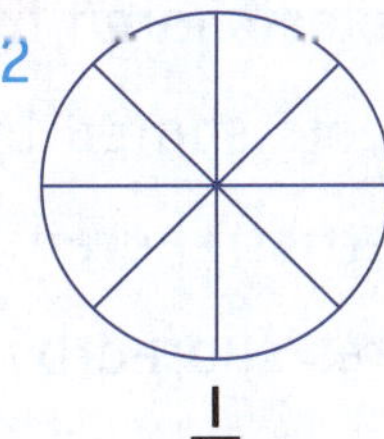
$\frac{1}{4}$

3 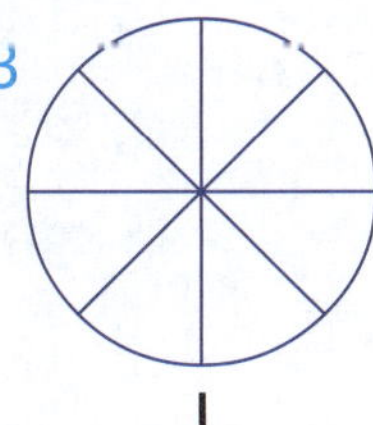
$\frac{1}{8}$

4 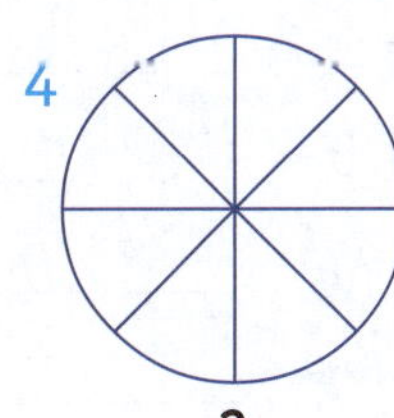
$\frac{3}{4}$

5 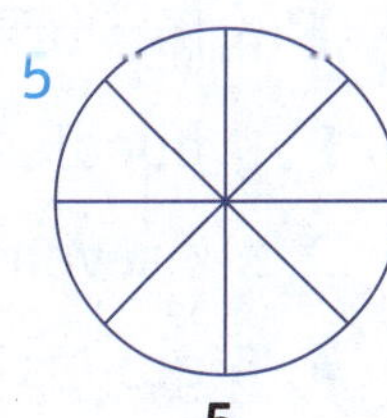
$\frac{5}{8}$

Draw lines and colour the fraction.

6 
$\frac{1}{5}$

7 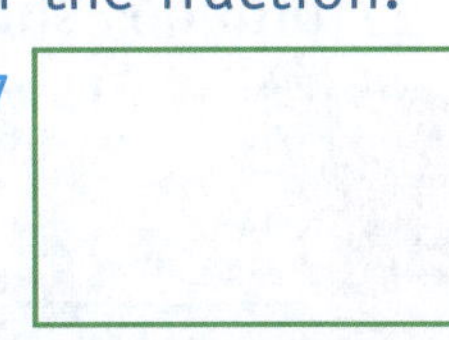
$\frac{1}{10}$

8 
$\frac{5}{10}$

9 
$\frac{4}{5}$

Score

Problem of the week
You can use a calculator.

34

42

Using three of the numbers each time make as many different totals as you can.
Write the totals here.

____

____

Unit 22

How many in each fair share?

A

1 24 in 2 shares ____
2 36 in 4 shares ____
3 18 in 3 shares ____
4 20 in 5 shares ____
5 36 in 6 shares ____
6 24 in 8 shares ____
7 21 in 3 shares ____
8 20 in 4 shares ____
9 42 in 6 shares ____
10 35 in 5 shares ____
11 54 in 2 shares ____
12 24 in 3 shares ____
13 25 in 5 shares ____
14 90 in 9 shares ____
15 16 in 4 shares ____
16 27 in 9 shares ____
17 40 in 5 shares ____
18 24 in 4 shares ____
19 30 in 3 shares ____
20 48 in 2 shares ____

Score

B

1 4 lots of 7 = ____
2 9 bundles of 5 = ____
3 six sevens = ____
4 6 groups of 8 = ____
5 two eights = ____
6 9 lots of 6 = ____
7 3 bundles of 7 = ____
8 8 groups of 4 = ____

How many in each?

9 15 apples shared by 3 ____
10 24 sweets shared by 4 ____
11 36 cherries shared by 9 ____
12 12 cakes shared by 3 ____
13 42 books shared by 7 ____
14 27 oranges shared by 3 ____

Score

C

1 70 = ____ tens
2 6 + ____ = 19
3 ____ − 11 = 19
4 ____ days in April
5 63 days = ____ weeks
6 9 × ____ = 81
7 3 + ____ − 4 = 9
8 21 − ____ = 4
9 48 hours = ____ days
10 2 L = 2000 ____
11 500 mL = ____ L
12 750 mL + ____ mL = 1 L
13 $2\frac{1}{2}$ hr = ____ min
14 ____ sec = $\frac{1}{2}$ min
15 3 months = ____ year

Score

Unit 22

Strategy
Split strategy for addition

eg 35 + 42 = 30 + 40 + 5 + 2
= 77

1 64 + 37 = ______
= ______

2 36 + 29 = ______
= ______

3 17 + 77 = ______
= ______

4 53 + 37 = ______
= ______

5 25 + 65 = ______
= ______

6 49 + 42 = ______
= ______

7 78 + 15 = ______
= ______

8 85 + 24 = ______
= ______

Score

Fair shares

Make fair shares. How many in each share?

1 4 fair shares ______
2 6 fair shares ______
3 2 fair shares ______
4 12 fair shares ______
5 18 fair shares ______
6 9 fair shares ______
7 36 fair shares ______
8 3 fair shares ______

Measurement

Make a list of tools that are used to measure length.

______ ______ ______
______ ______ ______
______ ______ ______

Problem of the week

4, 5, 6 are next-door numbers.

Use next-door numbers to make these true.

1 ◯ + ◯ + ◯ = 9
2 ◯ + ◯ + ◯ + ◯ = 18
3 ◯ + ◯ + ◯ = 24
4 ◯ + ◯ + ◯ + ◯ = 38

Unit 23

A

1 16 − 8 = ______
2 23 − 7 = ______
3 17 − 7 = ______
4 24 − 9 = ______
5 19 − 7 = ______
6 23 − 4 = ______
7 17 − 9 = ______
8 20 − 8 = ______
9 18 − 6 = ______
10 23 − 8 = ______
11 21 − 4 = ______
12 19 − 4 = ______
13 25 − 7 = ______
14 16 − 5 = ______
15 15 − 9 = ______
16 27 − 9 = ______
17 22 − 5 = ______
18 20 − 11 = ______
19 26 − 8 = ______
20 18 − 9 = ______

Score

Fill in the missing term.

B

1 2, 4, 6, ______ , 10
2 12, 15, ______ , 21, 24
3 60, 55, 50, 45, ______
4 1, 2, 4, 8, ______ , 32
5 80, 40, ______ , 10, 5
6 3, ______ , 7, 9, 11
7 9, 18, 27, 36, ______
8 2, 8, 14, ______ ,26
9 20, 17, ______ , 11, 8
10 72, 63, 54, ______ , 36
11 1, 10, 100, ______ , 10 000
12 $\frac{1}{2}$, $\frac{1}{3}$, ______ , $\frac{1}{5}$, $\frac{1}{6}$
13 84, 82, 80, ______ , 76
14 71, 69, ______ ,65, 63
15 40, 33, 26, 19, ______

Score

C

1 share 24 between 6 ______
2 sum of 8 and 12 ______
3 difference between 90 and 70 ______
4 5 times zero ______
5 80c − 6c − 6c − 6c ______
6 6 apples at 7c each ______
7 $\frac{1}{2}$ m = ______ cm
8 $\frac{1}{2}$ L = ______ mL
9 $\frac{1}{2}$ of 120 = ______
10 $\frac{1}{4}$ of 120 = ______
11 $\frac{1}{4}$ of $10 = ______
12 days in 1 year = ______
13 months in 2 years = ______
14 17 plus 4 lots of 4 = ______
15 At noon it is ______ o'clock.

Score

Strategy

Multiplying by 8

×4 then double eg $7 \times 8 = (7 \times 4) \times 2 = 56$

OR double, double, double eg $7 \times 8 = (14 \times 2) \times 2 = 56$

×4 then double	double, double, double	
1 $6 \times 8 =$ ____	6 $4 \times 8 =$ ____	11 $0 \times 8 =$ ____
2 $2 \times 8 =$ ____	7 $8 \times 8 =$ ____	12 $100 \times 8 =$ ____
3 $5 \times 8 =$ ____	8 $30 \times 8 =$ ____	13 $11 \times 8 =$ ____
4 $9 \times 8 =$ ____	9 $12 \times 8 =$ ____	14 $21 \times 8 =$ ____
5 $20 \times 8 =$ ____	10 $25 \times 8 =$ ____	15 $15 \times 8 =$ ____

Score

Calculator puzzle

Birth day and month

1 Multiply the number of your birth month by 5. =

2 Add 7. =

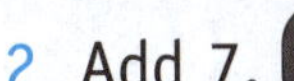

3 Multiply by 4. =

4 Add 13. =

5 Multiply by 5. =

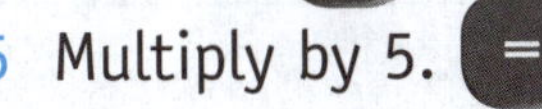

6 Add your birth day number. =

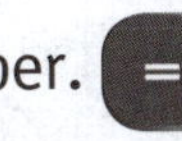

7 Subtract 205. =

The calculator will now show your birth month followed by your birth day.

eg

is 25th July

Try this on your family. They will think you are very clever.

Problem of the week

The faces of the cube are numbered in order.

1 What could the other faces be numbered?

____ ____ ____ ____

2 What could be the sum of the faces?

____ ____ ____ ____

Unit 24

A

1 $6 \times 6 =$ ______
2 $45 \div 5 =$ ______
3 $8 \times 9 =$ ______
4 $56 \div 7 =$ ______
5 $6 \times 7 =$ ______
6 $72 \div 9 =$ ______
7 $5 \times 5 =$ ______
8 $0 \times 6 =$ ______
9 $8 \times 7 =$ ______
10 $32 \div 4 =$ ______
11 $6 \times 8 =$ ______
12 $7 \div 7 =$ ______
13 $9 \times 4 =$ ______
14 $8 \times 8 =$ ______
15 $7 \times 5 =$ ______
16 $54 \div 6 =$ ______
17 $9 \times 3 =$ ______
18 $24 \div 8 =$ ______
19 $7 \times 7 =$ ______
20 $81 \div 9 =$ ______

Score

B True (T) or false (F).

1 $6 + 7 = 7 + 6$ ______
2 $10 - 8 = 8 - 10$ ______
3 $9 \times 4 = 4 \times 9$ ______
4 $6 + 8 + 4 = 4 + 6 + 8$ ______
5 $3 \times 2 \times 5 = 5 \times 2 \times 4$ ______
6 $6 + 4 - 8 = 8 - 6 + 4$ ______
7 $13 + 9 + 5 = 9 + 13 + 5$ ______
8 $42 \div 7 = 7 \div 42$ ______
9 $19 \times 0 = 0 \times 19$ ______
10 $63 \times 1 = 63 \div 1$ ______
11 $38 - 17 = 17 - 38$ ______
12 $8 \times 7 = 7 \times 8$ ______
13 $24 \div 2 = 2 \div 24$ ______
14 $64 - 34 = 34 - 64$ ______
15 $7 + 8 - 10 = 8 + 7 - 10$ ______

Score

C Use a chance word – certain (C), possible (P), impossible (I).

1 There are eight days this week. ______
2 Sunday will follow Saturday. ______
3 It will rain next week. ______
4 All my hair will fall out. ______
5 I will wear glasses in the future. ______
6 The baby will be a boy or a girl. ______
7 The dog will speak English. ______
8 The hen will lay an egg. ______
9 Write something that will definitely happen. ______
10 Write something that is very likely to happen. ______
11 Write something that definitely will not happen. ______

Score

Unit 24

Strategy
Multiply by 6

Multiply by 3, then multiply by 2.
eg 3 x 6 = 3 x 3 x 2 = 9 x 2 = 18

1 4 x 6 = ______
= ______

2 5 x 6 = ______
= ______

3 6 x 6 = ______
= ______

4 7 x 6 = ______
= ______

5 8 x 6 = ______
= ______

6 9 x 6 = ______
= ______

7 30 x 6 = ______
= ______

8 50 x 6 = ______
= ______

Score

Number Muncher

This machine changes numbers twice.

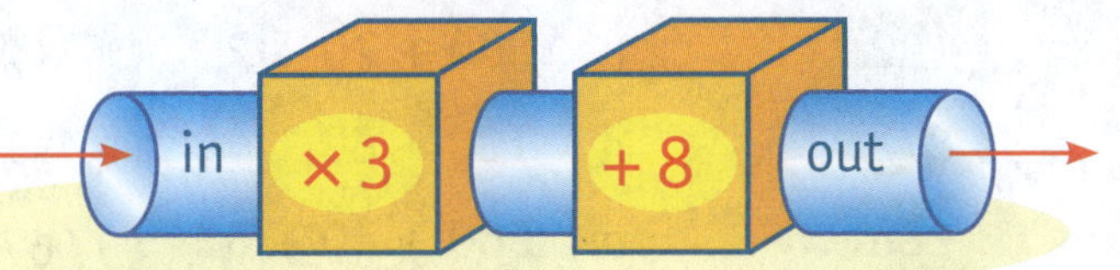

How do these numbers come out?

1 7 ______ 2 9 ______ 3 10 ______ 4 20 ______ 5 100 ______

Patterns

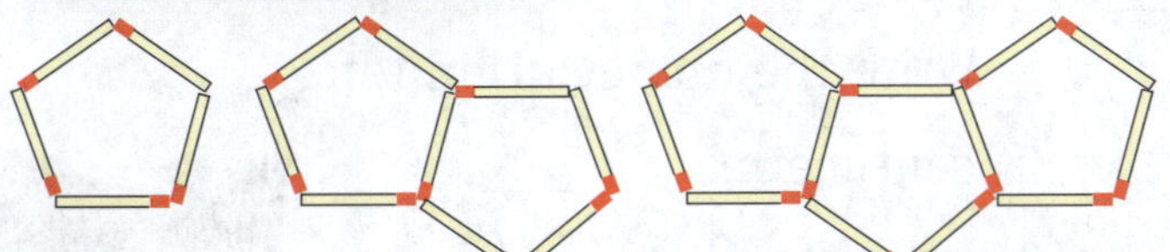

1 Draw the 5th term.

2 How many matches? ______

3 How many matches in the 8th term? ______

Problem of the week

Kelly was born in 1995.

When she turns 30 television will be 100 years old.

When did John Logie Baird demonstrate the first TV set?

______

Unit 25

A

1. 7 + 9 − 8 = ______
2. 15 − 9 + 7 = ______
3. 14 − 9 + 3 = ______
4. 6 + 8 − 7 = ______
5. 18 − 9 + 2 = ______
6. 8 + 5 − 6 = ______
7. 11 − 7 + 9 = ______
8. 11 − 3 + 8 = ______
9. 7 + 8 − 6 = ______
10. 13 − 4 + 7 = ______
11. 6 + 9 − 12 = ______
12. 17 − 8 + 11 = ______
13. 19 − 6 + 7 = ______
14. 12 − 4 + 12 = ______
15. 15 − 5 + 8 = ______
16. 16 − 7 + 5 = ______
17. 6 + 5 − 11 = ______
18. 20 − 12 + 6 = ______
19. 15 − 7 + 5 = ______
20. 8 + 3 − 9 = ______

Score

B Join matching pairs.

1	457	a	100 + 90 + 2
2	780	b	400 + 50 + 7
3	192	c	800 + 70 + 2
4	872	d	700 + 80
5	286	e	600 + 40 + 3
6	539	f	200 + 30 + 6
7	302	g	500 + 30 + 9
8	643	h	300 + 2

Use >, < or =,

9. 4789 ______ 7894
10. 8792 ______ 8792
11. 1290 ______ 1280
12. 3409 ______ 3490
13. 6782 ______ 6582
14. 5129 ______ 5029
15. 2484 ______ 4284

Score

C Circle the heavier item.

1	apple	cherry
2	chair	cushion
3	cat	horse
4	baby	doll
5	car	bus
6	bicycle	skateboard
7	sock	shoe
8	pen	pencil case

Write the abbreviation for:

9. centimetre. ______
10. millilitre. ______
11. millimetre. ______
12. litre. ______
13. kilogram. ______
14. metre. ______
15. gram. ______

Score

Unit 25

Strategy
To multiply by 5

Multiply by 10 and halve.
eg $14 \times 5 = 14 \times 10\ (140) \div 2 = 70$

1 $12 \times 5 =$ ______
2 $16 \times 5 =$ ______
3 $18 \times 5 =$ ______
4 $20 \times 5 =$ ______
5 $13 \times 5 =$ ______
6 $19 \times 5 =$ ______
7 $17 \times 5 =$ ______
8 $15 \times 5 =$ ______
9 $30 \times 5 =$ ______
10 $25 \times 5 =$ ______
11 $28 \times 5 =$ ______
12 $23 \times 5 =$ ______

Score

Symmetry

Draw all lines of symmetry.

1 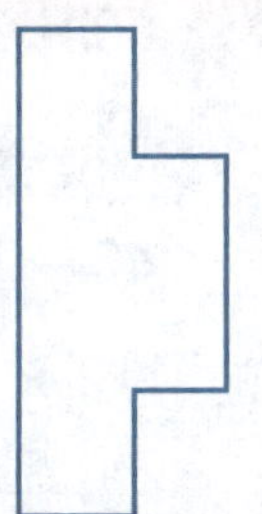

2 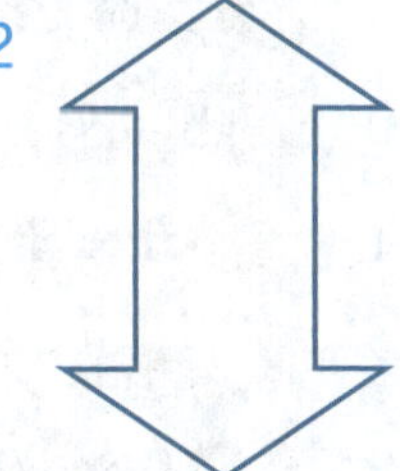

3 

4 

Mass

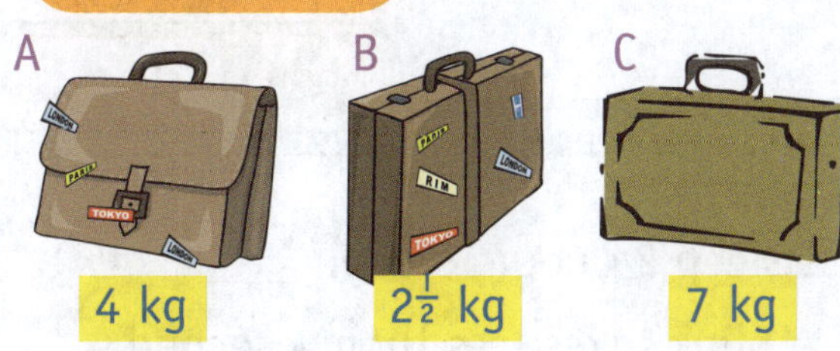

1 Write the briefcases from lightest to heaviest.

______

2 How many grams does each case weigh?

A ______ B ______

C ______

Problem of the week

The Smith's garden tap was dripping. It filled a 10 L bucket every 6 hours. How much water was lost in the 2 whole days they had to wait for the plumber to fix it?

______

Unit 26

A

1	16 + 11 = ____	8	19 + 13 = ____	15	15 + 12 = ____
2	14 + 12 = ____	9	14 + 16 = ____	16	19 + 11 = ____
3	17 + 10 = ____	10	11 + 17 = ____	17	16 + 15 = ____
4	15 + 14 = ____	11	18 + 15 = ____	18	13 + 16 = ____
5	18 + 13 = ____	12	14 + 14 = ____	19	23 + 14 = ____
6	12 + 12 = ____	13	12 + 16 = ____	20	25 + 12 = ____
7	13 + 15 = ____	14	17 + 12 = ____		

Score

Draw lines to match equal terms.

B

1	6 × 7	a	3 × 4	9	$\frac{1}{4}$ of 28	i	60 – 31
2	19 – 7	b	100 – 19	10	15 + 9 + 5	j	4 × 8
3	3 × 0	c	36 + 6	11	6 × 8	k	42 – 35
4	9 × 9	d	28 – 15 – 13	12	$\frac{1}{2}$ of 64	l	12 × 4
5	24 – 8	e	9 × 6	13	10 × 10	m	$\frac{4}{100}$
6	60 – 40 – 12	f	4 × 4	14	$\frac{1}{10}$ of 90	n	6 + 8 – 5
7	36 + 18	g	$\frac{1}{2}$ of 40	15	0·04	o	56 + 44
8	4 + 7 + 9	h	19 – 11				

Score

True (T) or false (F).

C

1 The classroom door is 1 m high. ____
2 My finger is about 15 cm. ____
3 The cup holds about 200 mL. ____
4 I buy milk by the litre. ____
5 A pencil is about 16 cm long. ____
6 A bucket can hold 10 L. ____
7 A year has 200 Saturdays. ____
8 June comes before April. ____
9 I sleep 24 hours a day. ____
10 A blink takes less than 1 second. ____
11 The $20 note is green. ____
12 The $1 coin is gold in colour. ____
13 Our car is 10 m long. ____
14 My nose is 5 mm long. ____
15 I will get this whole page correct. ____

Score

Unit 26

Strategy
Compensation strategy

eg 27 + 29 = 27 + 30 − 1 = 56 or 43 + 38 = 43 + 40 − 2 = 81

1 16 + 19 = ______
2 42 + 18 = ______
3 27 + 29 = ______
4 24 + 28 = ______
5 39 + 19 = ______
6 25 + 39 = ______
7 18 + 19 = ______
8 45 + 28 = ______
9 41 + 37 = ______
10 37 + 17 = ______
11 19 + 38 = ______
12 14 + 49 = ______
13 23 + 18 = ______
14 38 + 29 = ______
15 35 + 17 = ______

Score

Measurement

1 Measure these lines in mm.

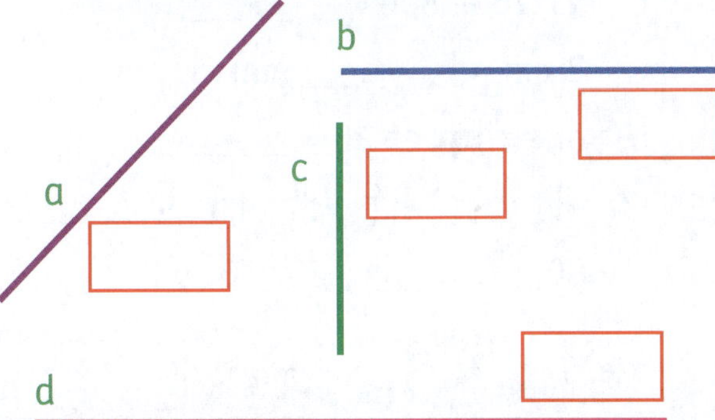

2 Draw these lines.
a 5 cm b 3 cm c $2\frac{1}{2}$ cm d 7 cm

Space 3D

These are views from the top.
What are they?

1

2

Problem of the week

Last week I piled some books into equal groups. There were 48 books. I can't remember the groups.

What could they have been?
eg 2 groups of 24. (2 × 24)

Unit 27 Revision

A

1 $9 \times 8 =$ ________
2 $8 + 4 + 9 =$ ________
3 $16 + 14 =$ ________
4 $24 - 8 =$ ________
5 $6 \times 9 =$ ________
6 $17 - 9 =$ ________
7 $3 \times 4 =$ ________
8 $4 \times 8 =$ ________
9 $21 - 11 =$ ________
10 $7 + 6 + 3 =$ ________
11 $22 - 7 - 12 =$ ________
12 $8 \times 0 =$ ________
13 $15 - 12 + 7 =$ ________
14 $17 + 12 =$ ________
15 $20 - 12 =$ ________
16 $15 + 6 - 9 =$ ________
17 $7 \times 6 =$ ________
18 $3 \times 3 \times 3 =$ ________
19 $25 + 7 + 4 =$ ________
20 $3 \times 8 - 20 =$ ________

Score

B

1 one quarter of 36 = ________
2 14, 17, 20, ________, 26
3 $6 + 6 + 6 + 6 + 6 + 6 =$ ________
4 $7 + 9 =$ ________ $\times 8$
5 90c + 40c = ________
6 81 cakes into 9 shares. 1 share = ________
7 $\frac{1}{2}$ of 48 = ________
8 70c + 45c = ________
9 $\frac{1}{2} =$ ________ quarters
10 9 equal shares of \$5 each = ________
11 \$1.75 + 80c = ________
12 2 cm = ________ mm
13 one fifth of 25 = ________
14 卌 卌 卌 卌 卌 || ________
15 80, ________, 20, 10, 5

Score

C

1 80 = ________ tens
2 7 bananas at 6c each ________
3 2 days = ________ hours
4 84c to the nearest 5c ________
5 share 36 between 9 ________
6 My finger is about ________ cm long.
7 4 + ________ − 7 = 10
8 $\frac{1}{2} = \frac{\square}{8}$
9 \$1.55 to the nearest dollar ________
10 40 mm = ________ cm
11 2 L = ________ mL
12 3 hours = ________ minutes
13 $3\frac{1}{2}$ m = ________ cm
14 $\frac{1}{4}$ of \$10 = ________
15 55 mm = ________ cm

Score

Revision

Unit 27

Strategy

Use the strategies you have learnt.

1 38 + 53 = ______

2 22 + 49 = ______

3 56 + 17 = ______

4 64 − 26 = ______

5 37 − 19 = ______

6 8 × 8 = ______

7 12 × 8 = ______

8 4 × 14 = ______

= ______

9 5 × 19 = ______

= ______

10 5 × 30 = ______

11 9 × 30 = ______

12 23 + 9 = ______

23 + 19 = ______

Score

Space

Colour the pentagon blue, the quadrilaterals red and the hexagon green.

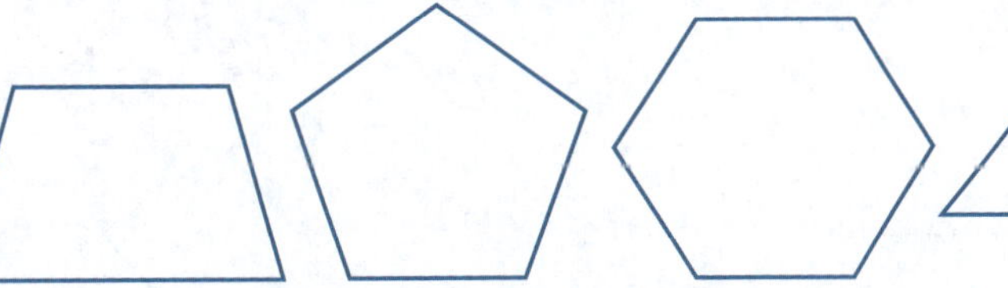

Fractions

Colour:

1

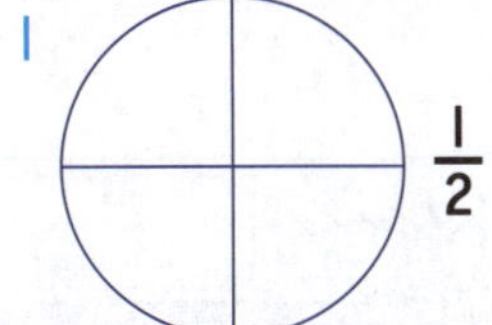

$\frac{1}{2}$

2

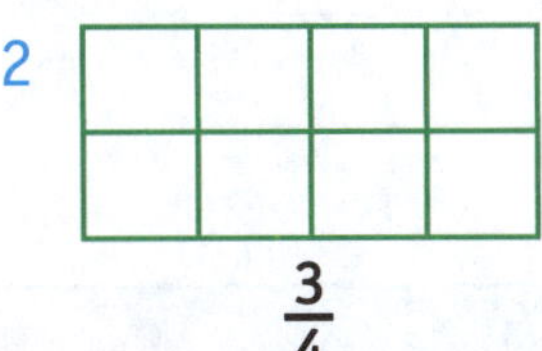

$\frac{3}{4}$

3

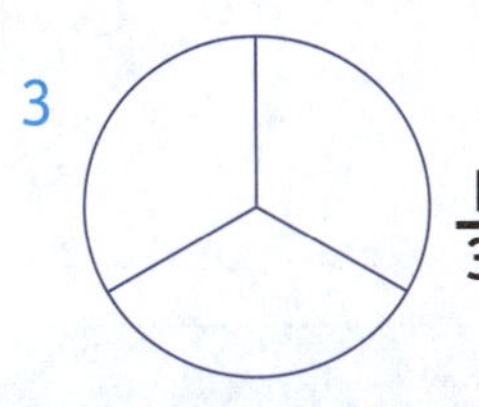

$\frac{1}{3}$

4

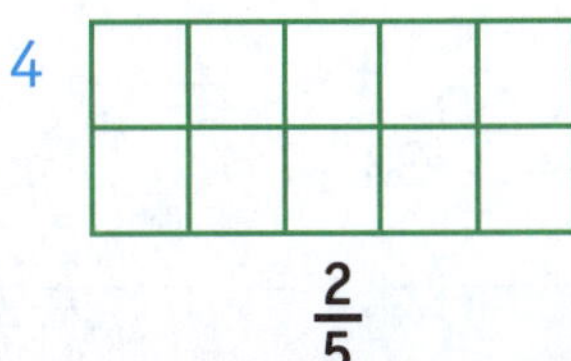

$\frac{2}{5}$

Measurement

Measure in mm.

1

2

Draw lines.

3 4 cm

4 $2\frac{1}{2}$ cm

Money

I bought a hat for $16 and socks for $7.50.

1 How much did I spend?

______

2 How much change would I get from $30?

______

Unit 28

A

1 7 + 2 + 8 = ______
2 3 + 5 + 4 = ______
3 9 + 2 + 6 = ______
4 5 + 7 + 3 = ______
5 7 + 9 + 6 = ______
6 6 + 4 + 7 = ______
7 8 + 6 + 6 = ______
8 6 + 9 + 7 = ______
9 8 + 2 + 5 = ______
10 5 + 8 + 8 = ______
11 7 + 3 + 9 = ______
12 9 + 5 + 7 = ______
13 8 + 8 + 8 = ______
14 6 + 7 + 6 = ______
15 8 + 9 + 5 = ______
16 6 + 8 + 5 = ______
17 7 + 4 + 8 = ______
18 9 + 9 + 4 = ______
19 5 + 5 + 4 = ______
20 7 + 8 + 6 = ______

Score

B Write to the nearest 10.

1 71 ______
2 27 ______
3 54 ______
4 85 ______
5 48 ______
6 62 ______
7 16 ______
8 33 ______

9 518
10 570
11 509
12 549
13 562
14 527
15 581

Write each number to the nearest 100.

9 ______
10 ______
11 ______
12 ______
13 ______
14 ______
15 ______

Score

C Use >, =, <.

1 6 + 8 ______ 7 × 2
2 23 − 9 ______ 5 + 8
3 7 × 6 ______ 8 × 5
4 9 × 0 ______ 2 × 5
5 32 + 8 ______ 26 + 14
6 3 × 2 × 5 ______ 76 − 44
7 10 × 10 ______ 54 + 44
8 3 + 18 + 10 ______ 50 − 21

9 How many in a score? ______
10 How many in 3 dozen? ______
11 How many years in a decade? ______
12 How many days in April? ______
13 How many weeks in 1 year? ______
14 How many months in a decade? ______
15 How many millilitres in 2 litres? ______

Score

Strategy

Jump strategy for + and –

76 + 19 = 76 + 10 + 9 (86 + 9)
= 95

76 – 19 = 76 – 10 – 9 (66 – 9)
= 57

1 43 + 15 = ______
= ______

2 43 – 15 = ______
= ______

3 38 + 26 = ______
= ______

4 38 – 26 = ______
= ______

5 34 + 27 = ______
= ______

6 34 – 27 = ______
= ______

7 54 + 29 = ______
= ______

8 54 – 29 = ______
= ______

Score

Number

1 Place these letters on the number line.

A = 2500 B = 3800 C = 4750 D = 120

0 5000

2 Write the value of each letter.

A D C E B

1000 2000

A = ______
B = ______
C = ______
D = ______
E = ______

Problem of the week

Last year Tony played tennis once per month and Maria played tennis 3 times per month. Together they played half the number of games the average tennis player plays.

How many games does the average tennis player play in 1 year?

______

Unit 29

A

1 7 × 2 = ______
2 10 × 7 = ______
3 0 × 7 = ______
4 7 × 6 = ______
5 4 × 7 = ______
6 7 × 3 = ______
7 7 × 10 = ______
8 7 × 7 = ______
9 8 × 7 = ______
10 2 × 7 = ______
11 7 × 4 = ______
12 9 × 7 = ______
13 5 × 7 = ______
14 7 × 0 = ______
15 7 × 1 = ______
16 6 × 7 = ______
17 7 × 8 = ______
18 7 × 5 = ______
19 3 × 7 = ______
20 7 × 9 = ______

Score

B Colour the multiples of 7.

1

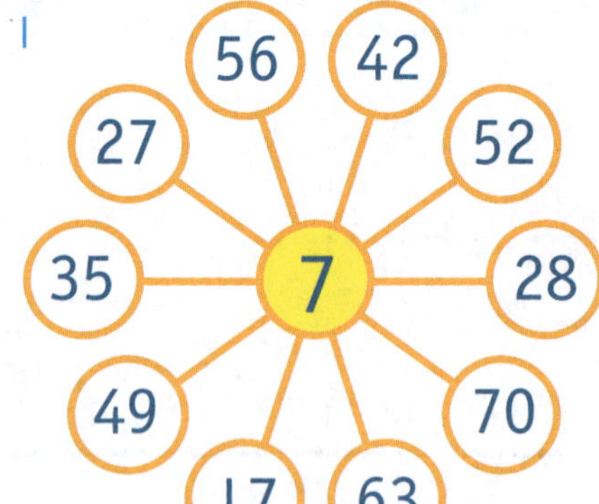

Colour the multiples of 8.

2

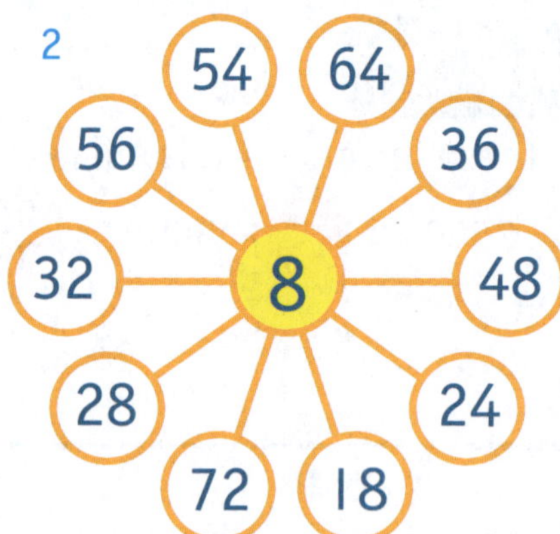

Score

C How many?

1 5c in 40c ______
2 10c in $3 ______
3 50c in $10 ______
4 20c in $1 ______
5 5c in $1 ______
6 10c in $1.50 ______
7 20c in $2.20 ______
8 50c in $100 ______
9 product of 3 and 7 ______
10 sum of 19 and 11 ______
11 difference between 20 and 6 ______
12 total 5, 6 and 12 ______
13 product of 2, 4 and 5 ______
14 subtract 12 from 18 ______
15 six times nine ______

Score

Strategy

Multiply by 9

Multiply by 3, then multiply by 3.
eg 4 × 9 = 4 × 3 × 3 = 12 x 3 = 36

1 3 × 9 = ____________
= ______

2 5 × 9 = ____________
= ______

3 6 × 9 = ____________
= ______

4 7 × 9 = ____________
= ______

5 8 × 9 = ____________
= ______

6 9 × 9 = ____________
= ______

Score

Multiplication

Write as many multiplication facts as you can for this group of mushrooms. eg 1 × 36 = 36

____

____

____

____

Time

JULY						
S	M	T	W	T	F	S
				1	2	3
4	5	6	7	8	9	10
11	12	13	14	15	16	17
18	19	20	21	22	23	24
25	26	27	28	29	30	31

1 What day is 13th July? ____________

2 What date is the second Friday? ____________

3 How many Sundays in July? ____________

4 What was the last day of June? ____________

5 What was the first day of August? ____________

Problem of the week

Each shape has its own value less than 10. What are the values?

triangle + square = circle

circle − rectangle = pentagon

square × square = pentagon

pentagon − rectangle = triangle

Unit 30

A

1. 15 − 7 − 3 = ______
2. 23 − 8 − 9 = ______
3. 19 − 11 − 2 = ______
4. 21 − 9 − 5 = ______
5. 25 − 8 − 7 = ______
6. 20 − 12 − 6 = ______
7. 18 − 13 − 4 = ______
8. 20 − 7 − 6 = ______
9. 26 − 8 − 9 = ______
10. 24 − 9 − 5 = ______
11. 17 − 6 − 7 = ______
12. 15 − 10 − 5 = ______
13. 28 − 10 − 7 = ______
14. 32 − 5 − 5 = ______
15. 18 − 12 − 3 = ______
16. 12 − 9 − 1 = ______
17. 24 − 12 − 9 = ______
18. 30 − 8 − 5 = ______
19. 26 − 10 − 9 = ______
20. 25 − 9 − 10 = ______

Score

B Write a multiplication to solve:

1. 28 ÷ 4 ______
2. 36 ÷ 6 ______
3. 72 ÷ 8 ______
4. 45 ÷ 9 ______
5. 49 ÷ 7 ______
6. 81 ÷ 9 ______
7. 35 ÷ 5 ______
8. 42 ÷ 6 ______

How many:

9. 5c sweets for 45c? ______
10. 10c sweets for $1.00? ______
11. 7c sweets for 56c? ______
12. 9c sweets for 72c? ______
13. 8c sweets for 64c? ______
14. 6c sweets for 66c? ______
15. 9c sweets for 63c? ______

Score

C How many?

1. cm in 1 m ______
2. mm in 1 cm ______
3. mL in 1 L ______
4. days in 3 school weeks ______
5. eggs in 2 dozen ______
6. minutes in $\frac{3}{4}$ hour ______
7. hours in $\frac{1}{4}$ day ______
8. days in January ______
9. legs on 7 spiders ______
10. days in 7 weeks ______
11. months in 1 decade ______
12. years in 1 century ______
13. 5c coins in $1 ______
14. $2 coins in $20 ______
15. mL in $\frac{1}{2}$ L ______

Score

Strategy
Counting on for subtraction

53 – 48 → Count on (49, 50, 51, 52, 53) = 5

53 – 48 = 5

1 34 – 29 = ______	5 80 – 73 = ______	9 46 – 38 = ______
2 51 – 44 = ______	6 93 – 86 = ______	10 62 – 58 = ______
3 65 – 58 = ______	7 55 – 49 = ______	11 91 – 85 = ______
4 72 – 65 = ______	8 21 – 18 = ______	12 103 – 97 = ______

Score

Calculator

Use a calculator for these.

1 A heart is beating 84 times per minute. How many times will it beat in an hour? ______

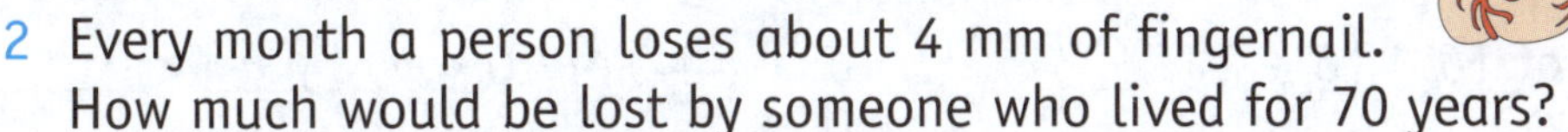

2 Every month a person loses about 4 mm of fingernail. How much would be lost by someone who lived for 70 years? ______

3 A foot contains 26 bones. How many bones would be in the feet of 250 people? ______

Time

Write these times in words.

1 

______

2 03:05 ______

3 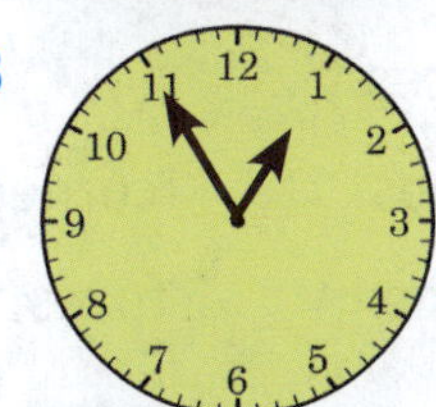

______

4 11:45 ______

Problem of the week

In class 3Z at Billaball School there are 24 students. $\frac{1}{4}$ order their lunch from the canteen, $\frac{1}{3}$ go home for lunch and the rest bring their lunch to school.

How many bring their lunch to school? ______

Unit 31

A

1 $48 \div 8 =$ ______
2 $80 \div 8 =$ ______
3 $14 \div 7 =$ ______
4 $42 \div 7 =$ ______
5 $56 \div 7 =$ ______
6 $8 \div 8 =$ ______
7 $72 \div 8 =$ ______
8 $49 \div 7 =$ ______
9 $16 \div 8 =$ ______
10 $28 \div 7 =$ ______
11 $64 \div 8 =$ ______
12 $63 \div 7 =$ ______
13 $32 \div 8 =$ ______
14 $7 \div 7 =$ ______
15 $24 \div 8 =$ ______
16 $70 \div 7 =$ ______
17 $56 \div 8 =$ ______
18 $21 \div 7 =$ ______
19 $40 \div 8 =$ ______
20 $35 \div 7 =$ ______

Score

B Find the fraction.

1 $\frac{1}{3}$ of $15 = 15 \div 3 =$ ______
2 $\frac{1}{5}$ of $15 = 15 \div 5 =$ ______
3 $\frac{1}{2}$ of $16 = 16 \div 2 =$ ______
4 $\frac{1}{4}$ of $16 = 16 \div$ __ $=$ ______
5 $\frac{1}{8}$ of $16 = 16 \div$ __ $=$ ______
6 $\frac{1}{2}$ of $20 = 20 \div$ __ $=$ ______
7 $\frac{1}{4}$ of $20 =$ ______ $=$ ______
8 $\frac{1}{5}$ of $20 =$ ______ $=$ ______
9 $\frac{1}{10}$ of $20 =$ ______ $=$ ______
10 $\frac{1}{2}$ of $24 =$ ______ $=$ ______
11 $\frac{1}{4}$ of $24 =$ ______ $=$ ______
12 $\frac{1}{3}$ of $24 =$ ______ $=$ ______

Score

C True (T) or false (F).

1 A triangle has 3 angles. ______
2 A cube has 4 faces. ______
3 A pentagon has 6 sides. ______
4 A trapezium has 4 sides. ______
5 Parallel lines meet at right angles. ______
6 An octagon has 8 sides. ______
7 A quadrilateral has 4 angles. ______
8 A hexagon has 6 sides. ______

Complete.

9 A cone has a ______ base.
10 A tennis ball is like a ______.
11 A can of drink is like a ______.
12 A die has ______ faces.
13 A triangular prism has ______ corners.
14 A square pyramid has ______ faces.
15 This page is a ______.

Score

Unit 31

Strategy
Look for patterns

$5 \times 6 = 30$ so $6 \times 5 = 30$

$30 \div 5 = 6$

$30 \div 6 = 5$

Write three more facts for each.

1 $7 \times 8 = 56$ ______ ______ ______

2 $9 \times 4 = 36$ ______ ______ ______

3 $6 \times 9 = 54$ ______ ______ ______

4 $48 \div 6 = 8$ ______ ______ ______

5 $63 \div 7 = 9$ ______ ______ ______

Score

Space
Draw:

a a cone. b a sphere. c a cylinder.

Fractions
Colour to show:

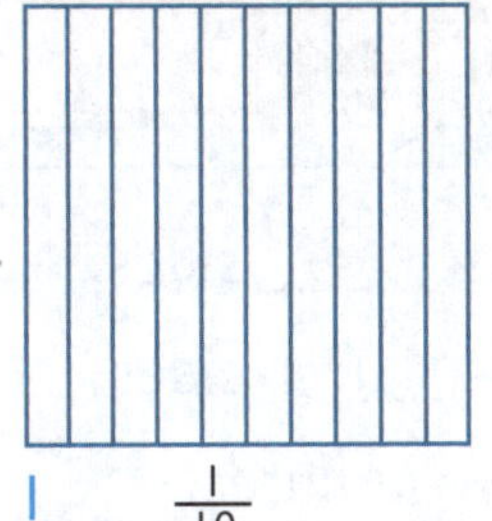

1 $\frac{1}{10}$

2 $\frac{9}{10}$

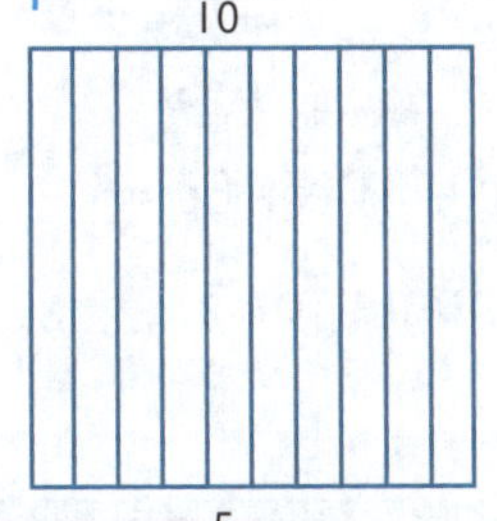

3 $\frac{5}{10}$

4 $\frac{3}{10}$

Problem of the week
Put all the eggs in their correct burrow.

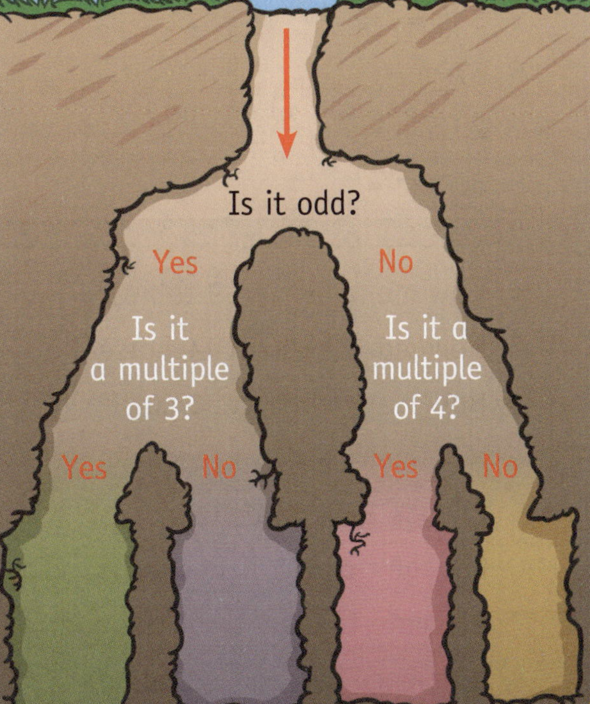

Unit 32

A

1 8 − 7 + 9 = ______
2 11 + 4 − 8 = ______
3 20 − 8 + 7 = ______
4 15 + 3 − 9 = ______
5 9 + 7 + 5 = ______
6 21 − 11 + 6 = ______
7 14 + 3 − 8 = ______
8 9 + 8 − 5 = ______
9 18 − 7 − 4 = ______
10 13 + 6 − 12 = ______
11 12 − 9 + 9 = ______
12 15 − 7 + 8 = ______
13 17 − 6 + 9 = ______
14 21 − 9 + 3 = ______
15 7 + 6 + 7 = ______
16 4 + 13 − 9 = ______
17 19 − 13 + 8 = ______
18 15 − 9 + 11 = ______
19 20 − 19 − 1 = ______
20 18 − 13 + 12 = ______

Score

B Change to metres (m).

1 200 cm = ______
2 700 cm = ______
3 900 cm = ______
4 450 cm = ______

Change to centimetres (cm).

5 3 m = ______
6 $6\frac{1}{2}$ m = ______
7 20 mm = ______
8 80 mm = ______

Change to millimetres (mm).

9 3 cm = ______
10 7 cm = ______
11 10 cm = ______
12 $1\frac{1}{2}$ cm = ______
13 1 cm 7 mm = ______ mm
14 1 m 42 cm = ______ cm
15 5 m 3 cm = ______ cm

Score

C

1 How many legs on 9 tables? ______
2 How many eyes on 14 horses? ______
3 How many ears on 30 cats? ______
4 How many legs on 7 dogs? ______
5 Change 315c to dollars. ______
6 Change from $5 if I spend $2.20. ______
7 Estimate the length of the board. ______
8 Difference between 32 cm and 50 cm. ______
9 A pentagon has ______ sides.
10 An octagon has ______ sides.
11 3 hours = ______ minutes.
12 November has ______ days.
13 20c + 20c + 50c + 10c + 5c = ______
14 Write another name for $\frac{1}{2}$. ______
15 $\frac{1}{5}$ of $1 = ______

Score

Strategy
Multiplying by teens

Multiply by 10 first.

eg 7 × 14 = 7 × 10 and 7 × 4
(= 70 + 28)
= 98

9 × 17 = 9 × 10 and 9 × 7
(= 90 + 63)
= 153

1 8 × 13 = ______
= ______

2 5 × 15 = ______
= ______

3 6 × 14 = ______
= ______

4 4 × 17 = ______
= ______

5 3 × 18 = ______
= ______

6 7 × 12 = ______
= ______

7 9 × 13 = ______
= ______

8 6 × 19 = ______
= ______

Score

Area

1 What is the area of A? ______ B? ______

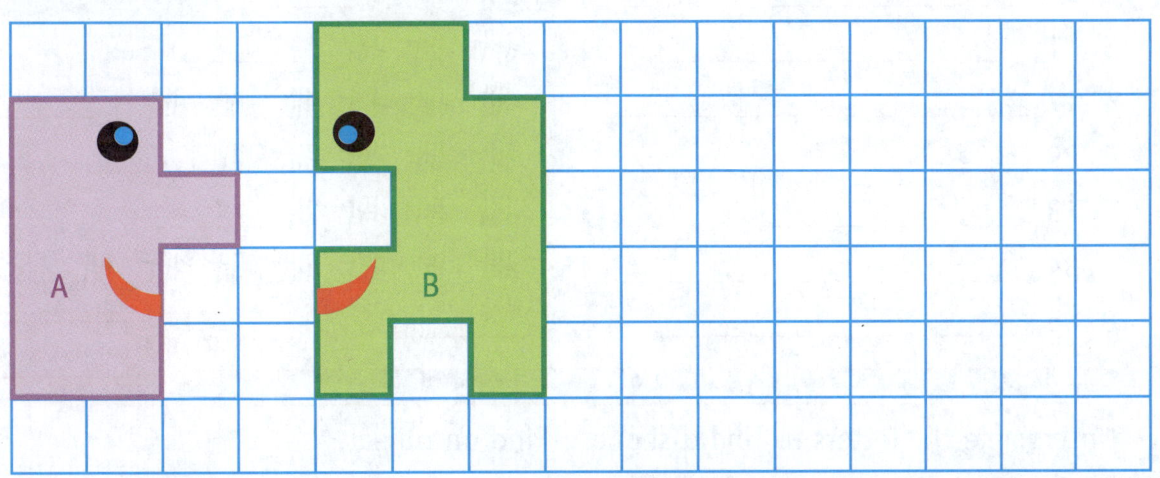

2 Draw 2 aliens with areas of 10 squares and 15 squares next to A and B.

Chance

Write an event that is likely to happen next month.

______

______

______

Problem of the week

Use the digits 1, 2, 3, 4, 5, 6 and 7 and addition signs to make 100.

Unit 33

A

1 3 × 7 = ______

2 9 × 9 = ______

3 8 × 6 = ______

4 5 × 5 = ______

5 0 × 4 = ______

6 3 × 8 = ______

7 8 × 10 = ______

8 4 × 6 = ______

9 7 × 9 = ______

10 6 × 9 = ______

11 7 × 6 = ______

12 9 × 8 = ______

13 4 × 8 = ______

14 6 × 6 = ______

15 10 × 10 = ______

16 5 × 9 = ______

17 8 × 5 = ______

18 9 × 7 = ______

19 7 × 0 = ______

20 6 × 3 = ______

Score

B Draw tally marks to show:

1 7 ______

2 9 ______

3 11 ______

4 17 ______

5 29 ______

6 13 ______

7 34 ______

8 46 ______

What numbers do these represent?

9 卌 ||| ______

10 卌 卌 || ______

11 卌 卌 卌 ______

12 卌 卌 卌 卌 卌 卌 | ______

13 卌 卌 卌 卌 |||| ______

14 卌 卌 卌 |||| ______

15 卌 卌 卌 卌 卌 卌 卌 卌 ______

Score

C Unscramble the letters to find a shape.

1 qrsuea ______

2 lericc ______

3 ctagnoo ______

4 exaoghn ______

5 urpezimat ______

6 hitgr lngea ______

7 gentopan ______

8 mellagraporal ______

Find an object.

9 once ______

10 rimps ______

11 drylinec ______

12 drymapi ______

13 buec ______

14 reepsh ______

15 quears prims ______

Score

Unit 33

Strategy
Multiply by 30

multiply by 3 and by 10 (add a zero)
eg $7 \times 30 = (7 \times 3) \times 10$
$= 210$

1 $8 \times 30 =$ ______
2 $6 \times 30 =$ ______
3 $9 \times 30 =$ ______
4 $3 \times 30 =$ ______
5 $2 \times 30 =$ ______
6 $5 \times 30 =$ ______
7 $4 \times 30 =$ ______
8 $10 \times 30 =$ ______
9 $11 \times 30 =$ ______
10 $20 \times 30 =$ ______

Score

Space

Circle right angles:

a

b
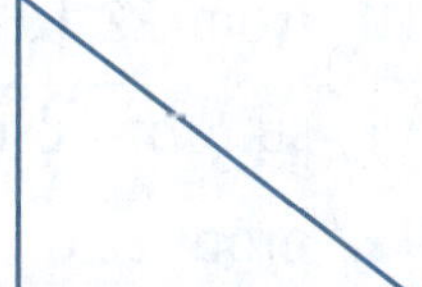
c

d

Position

6	D	O	R	D	E	H
5	A	N	L	R	U	S
4	L	T	I	S	A	O
3	R	M	E	U	N	A
2	W	O	A	D	Z	L
1	I	S	U	M	E	S
	1	2	3	4	5	6

What am I?

Use the letters in the grid to find the answer.

1 column 3 row 4
2 column 6 row 3
3 column 4 row 1
4 column 5 row 4
5 column 2 row 3
6 column 3 row 2
7 column 2 row 4
8 column 6 row 6
9 column 6 row 1
10 column 1 row 2
11 column 1 row 1
12 column 5 row 2

___ (1) ___ (2) ___ (3) ___ (4) ___ (5) ___ (6) ___ (7) ___ (8) ___ (9) ___ (10) ___ (11) ___ (12)

Problem of the week

The answer is 1. The numbers are 3, 6, 7, 10.

What is the question? ______

Unit 34

A

1 3 × 9 = ______
2 18 ÷ 2 = ______
3 6 × 7 = ______
4 40 ÷ 8 = ______
5 7 × 9 = ______
6 21 ÷ 3 = ______
7 9 × 9 = ______
8 5 ÷ 5 = ______
9 4 × 8 = ______
10 48 ÷ 6 = ______
11 8 × 8 = ______
12 16 ÷ 4 = ______
13 7 × 7 = ______
14 100 ÷ 10 = ______
15 5 × 6 = ______
16 56 ÷ 7 = ______
17 0 × 4 = ______
18 54 ÷ 6 = ______
19 1 × 9 = ______
20 28 ÷ 4 = ______

Score

B

1 product of 3 and 4 ______
2 sum of 12 and 6 ______
3 total of 3, 9, 4 and 2 ______
4 difference between 20 and 2 ______
5 16 minus 12 ______
6 8 lots of 4 ______
7 share 54 among 6 ______
8 10 times 16 ______
9 subtract 13 from 25 ______
10 from 22 take 17 ______
11 sum of 16 and 11 ______
12 product of 5 and 7 ______
13 total of 12 and 9 ______
14 minus 7 from 11 ______
15 from 40 take the product of 5 and 2 ______

Score

C True (T) or false (F).

1 A square has right angles. ______
2 100 g = 1 kg ______
3 7 pm is in the morning. ______
4 $\frac{1}{2} = \frac{4}{8}$ ______
5 $\frac{1}{2}$ L = 500 mL ______
6 April has 31 days. ______
7 36 = 3 dozen ______
8 $\frac{1}{3} > \frac{1}{2}$ ______
9 A pentagon has 6 angles. ______
10 A triangular prism has 5 faces. ______
11 399 > 501 ______
12 400 m = 4 cm ______
13 5:45 is $\frac{1}{4}$ to 6 ______
14 294c = $2.94 ______
15 $2 = five 20c coins ______

Score

Unit 34

Strategy
Finding tens

$$13 + 14 + 7 = 20 + 14$$
$$= 34$$

1 12 + 5 + 5 = ______

2 7 + 11 + 3 = ______

3 8 + 2 + 16 = ______

4 6 + 9 + 4 = ______

5 8 + 9 + 1 = ______

6 13 + 7 + 11 = ______

7 8 + 14 + 6 = ______

8 15 + 17 + 5 = ______

9 8 + 19 + 1 = ______

10 13 + 12 + 8 = ______

11 3 + 9 + 17 = ______

12 24 + 6 + 11 = ______

Score

Position

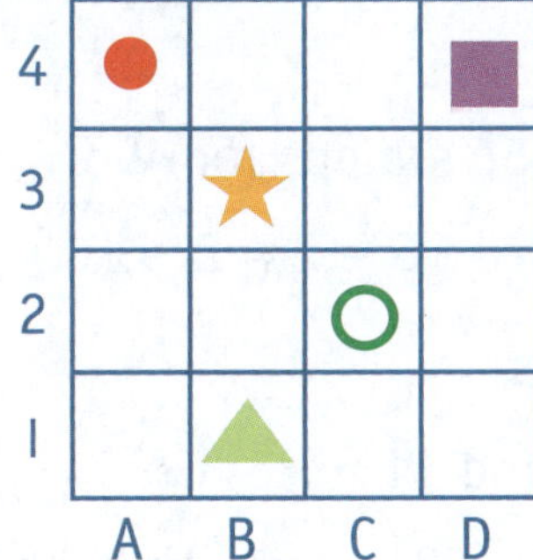

Where is the:

1 square? ______ 2 star? ______

3 circle? ______ 4 triangle? ______

5 What is at A4?

______

Direction

In what direction from Kev is the:

1 cake? ______ 2 iceblock? ______

2 pie? ______ 4 ice-cream? ______

Problem of the week

Sal, Kylie, Amanda, Charlie and Barry stand in a line. Sal is 3 places away from Charlie who is 2 places away from Barry. Amanda is next to Barry. Kylie likes to stand next to a boy. Write their names in the correct order.

______ ______ ______ ______ ______

Unit 35 Revision

A

1 $6 + 9 + 5 =$ ______
2 $0 \times 9 =$ ______
3 $13 + 9 - 11 =$ ______
4 $17 - 10 + 6 =$ ______
5 $7 \times 6 =$ ______
6 $21 - 6 - 11 =$ ______
7 $56 \div 8 =$ ______
8 $19 - 3 - 8 =$ ______
9 $17 + 13 =$ ______
10 $49 \div 7 =$ ______
11 $100 \div 10 =$ ______
12 $8 + 7 + 6 =$ ______
13 $9 \times 1 =$ ______
14 $16 \div 4 =$ ______
15 $54 \div 6 =$ ______
16 $17 + 2 - 8 =$ ______
17 $8 \times 8 =$ ______
18 $10 \times 10 =$ ______
19 $14 + 3 + 7 =$ ______
20 $23 - 15 - 7 =$ ______

Score

B

1 74 to the nearest 10 ______
2 159 to the nearest 100 ______
3 $\frac{4}{8} = \frac{1}{\square}$
4 $\frac{1}{5}$ of 30 = 30 ☐ 5
5 $6 + 7 =$ ______ $+ 6$
6 $3 \times 4 \times 10 = 10 \times$ ______ $\times 3$
7 $\frac{1}{2} = \frac{5}{\square}$
8 ______ $\times 6 = 6 \times 12$
9 next multiple of 3 after 20 ______
10 $5 \times$ ______ $= 0$
11 How many 5c stamps for 45c? ______
12 True or false? $16 \div 2 = 2 \div 16$ ______
13 $\frac{2}{4} = \frac{\square}{2}$
14 total 3, 9 and 11 ______
15 True or false. 28 is a multiple of 8. ______

Score

C

1 How many in a score? ______
2 How many years in a decade? ______
3 How many 5c in $1? ______
4 How many 10c in $1.60? ______
5 difference between 16 and 7 ______
6 A cube has ______ faces.
7 A quadrilateral has ______ sides.
8 day after Monday ______
9 short form of litre ______
10 How many in 2 dozen? ______
11 product of 8 and 7 ______
12 $10 – $2.75 = ______
13 How many legs on 20 dogs? ______
14 mL in $\frac{1}{2}$ L ______
15 month before January ______

Score

Revision

Unit 35

Strategy

Use the strategies you have learnt.

1 44 + 15 = ______

2 44 − 15 = ______

3 37 × 10 = ______

4 8 × 100 = ______

5 36 × 100 = ______

6 82 − 77 = ______

7 59 − 14 = ______

8 16 × 5 = ______

9 9 × 7 = ______

10 7 × ______ = 63

11 63 ÷ ______ = 7

12 ______ ÷ 9 = 7

Score

Number

Place these letters on the number line.

A = 200 B = 450 C = 50 D = 350 E = 95

0 ______________________________ 500

Space

Draw:

1 a cone.

2 a quadrilateral.

3 parallel lines.

4 a cube.

Time

Write these times in words.

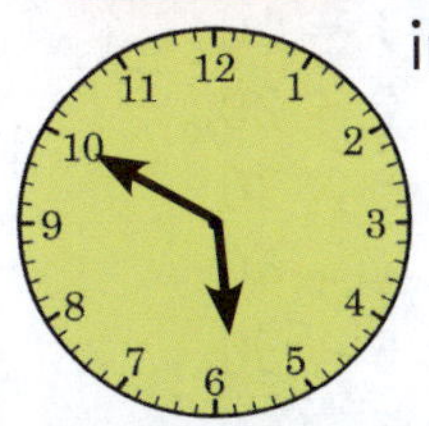

______

______

______

______

Position

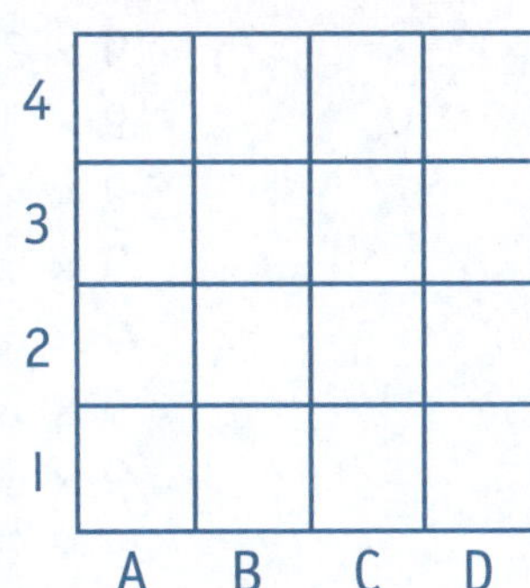

1 At A3 draw a star.

2 At C1 draw a square.

3 At B4 draw a triangle.

4 At D2 write X.

5 At A1 write your initial.

Multiplication tables

2× table

2 × 0 = 0
2 × 1 = 2
2 × 2 = 4
2 × 3 = 6
2 × 4 = 8
2 × 5 = 10
2 × 6 = 12
2 × 7 = 14
2 × 8 = 16
2 × 9 = 18
2 × 10 = 20

3× table

3 × 0 = 0
3 × 1 = 3
3 × 2 = 6
3 × 3 = 9
3 × 4 = 12
3 × 5 = 15
3 × 6 = 18
3 × 7 = 21
3 × 8 = 24
3 × 9 = 27
3 × 10 = 30

4× table

4 × 0 = 0
4 × 1 = 4
4 × 2 = 8
4 × 3 = 12
4 × 4 = 16
4 × 5 = 20
4 × 6 = 24
4 × 7 = 28
4 × 8 = 32
4 × 9 = 36
4 × 10 = 40

5× table

5 × 0 = 0
5 × 1 = 5
5 × 2 = 10
5 × 3 = 15
5 × 4 = 20
5 × 5 = 25
5 × 6 = 30
5 × 7 = 35
5 × 8 = 40
5 × 9 = 45
5 × 10 = 50

6× table

6 × 0 = 0
6 × 1 = 6
6 × 2 = 12
6 × 3 = 18
6 × 4 = 24
6 × 5 = 30
6 × 6 = 36
6 × 7 = 42
6 × 8 = 48
6 × 9 = 54
6 × 10 = 60

7× table

7 × 0 = 0
7 × 1 = 7
7 × 2 = 14
7 × 3 = 21
7 × 4 = 28
7 × 5 = 35
7 × 6 = 42
7 × 7 = 49
7 × 8 = 56
7 × 9 = 63
7 × 10 = 70

8× table

8 × 0 = 0
8 × 1 = 8
8 × 2 = 16
8 × 3 = 24
8 × 4 = 32
8 × 5 = 40
8 × 6 = 48
8 × 7 = 56
8 × 8 = 64
8 × 9 = 72
8 × 10 = 80

9× table

9 × 0 = 0
9 × 1 = 9
9 × 2 = 18
9 × 3 = 27
9 × 4 = 36
9 × 5 = 45
9 × 6 = 54
9 × 7 = 63
9 × 8 = 72
9 × 9 = 81
9 × 10 = 90

10× table

10 × 0 = 0
10 × 1 = 10
10 × 2 = 20
10 × 3 = 30
10 × 4 = 40
10 × 5 = 50
10 × 6 = 60
10 × 7 = 70
10 × 8 = 80
10 × 9 = 90
10 × 10 = 100